HERESIES

the
BIBLE
FOR
TODAY

900 Park Avenue
Collingswood, NJ 08108
Phone: 856-854-4452

BFT #595

Printed in the United States of America

ISBN 1-56848-014-8

THEOLOGICAL

HERESIES

OF WESTCOTT & HORT

PASTOR D. A. WAITE, TH.D., PH.D.

Dean John William Burgon
(1813—1888)
A Conservative Anglican Minister

History of the Book

In January 1978, the author published this study in a mimeograph format. In that form, it was thirty-eight pages in length, including the Table of Contents. Then, in May 1979, due to various requests for the material, the material was put in a booklet form. Finally, in June 1998, we enlarged the print from about nine point to ten point type and included an *Index of Words and Phrases* as well as a *Scripture Index* to make it more useful to the readers. This book has already been read by many thousands of readers in many parts of the world.

Regardless of what side one takes concerning the **Westcott and Hort** textual criticism of the **Traditional Greek Text** which underlies our **Authorized (King James) Version** of 1611, I believe it is of the utmost importance to see once and for all that **the leaders** in the **textual revolution** which unseated the **Traditional Received Greek Text** from its place of undisputed prominence for over **fifteen centuries**, were **not**, as most of the evangelical and fundamentalist world today believes, **fundamentalists**, or even **orthodox** in many of their beliefs. It is my personal belief that this **heterodoxy** on their part **blinded** their intellects, and prejudiced them adversely and unfairly in their **textual theories** of the Greek New Testament.

For proof of the above conclusion, we offer the following original study of **125 direct quotations from over 1,291 pag-**

es as contained in **five** books by both **Brooke Foss Westcott** and **Fenton John Anthony Hort**. The symbol for **poison** has been used throughout this book.

Bishop B. F. Westcott
(1825—1901)

Professor F. J. A. Hort
(1828—1892)

Two Liberal Anglican Ministers

Dedication

This book is dedicated to my wife since 1948, Yvonne S. Waite, who has sacrificed my presence during the research and writing of this and other studies; to my mother-in-law, Gertrude G. Sanborn, who gave me the first book to read on the Received Greek Text; and to my father-in-law, Ren O. Sanborn, who also expressed a great interest in the issue of the proper New Testament Greek Text.

Table of Contents

Chapter II
The Theological Heresies of Westcott and Hort
in Bibliology

Chapter III
The Theological Heresies of Westcott and Hort
in Theology Proper

Chapter IV
The Theological Heresies of Westcott and Hort in Anthropology and Hamartiology

Chapter V
The Theological Heresies of Westcott and Hort in Satanology

Chapter VI
The Theological Heresies of Westcott and Hort
in Ecclesiology

Chapter VII
The Theological Heresies of Westcott and Hort
in Pneumatology

Chapter VIII
The Theological Heresies of Westcott and Hort
in Eschatology

Chapter IX
The Theological Heresies of Westcott and Hort
in Soteriology

Chapter X
The Theological Heresies of Westcott and Hort
in Christology

Chapter XI
Summary and Conclusions

Chapter I
Background Information

Before beginning the analysis of the *Theological Heresies of Westcott and Hort,* I want to cover a few introductory matters which form a part of the background information for this study.

A. Why study Westcott and Hort's theological heresies? You might be asking the question, "Why should we study the theological heresies of Westcott and Hort?" This is a good question. First of all, it must be understood that Bishop Brooke Foss Westcott and Professor Fenton John Anthony Hort were the prime movers in the construction of an elaborate, yet fictitious, system of New Testament Greek *Textual Criticism* leading to an abandonment of the **Received** *New Testament Greek Text* in favor of a **Revised** *New Testament Greek Text.* This text, in turn, formed the basis for the 1881 *English Revised Version* (E.R.V.).

If these two Anglican churchmen are found to have espoused various and sundry *theological heresies,* then, most assuredly, those fundamentalists and even neo-evangelicals today should know about it, especially those who have ac-

cepted all or part of the *Westcott* and *Hort* system of manu-
script authority. This system is a worship of two documents,
the Vatican ("B") and the Sinai ("Aleph"). It makes use of an
introspective subjectivism in dealing with the verbally and
plenarily inspired and hence inerrant and infallible Word of
God.

If, however, it can be shown that *Westcott* and *Hort* were
fundamentalists and Bible-believers without so much as a taint
of *heresy* or of *apostasy*, then this is a different matter. If a
fundamentalist is following a *heretic*, he should know about
it, should he not? So, there is an *informational reason* for
such a study at the very least.

**B. What if Westcott and Hort had theological heresies, so
what?** Since *Westcott* and *Hort* are both quite largely vener-
ated as the *idols* of the *New Testament textual criticism world*,
and since these two men (principally *Hort*, however) were
the inventors of a doctored Greek text made up largely from
their worship of the Vatican ("B") and the Sinai ("Aleph")
manuscripts, this gives these two men great prominence in
the New Testament Greek field. Now it is to be recognized
that many N.T. textual critics today have discarded some of
the *Westcott–Hort* fabric of error. This does *not*, however, take
away the importance historically of these men in building
enough of a fire under the Received Text (Textus Receptus)
on which the King James Version was built to the extent of
seeking to *replace* that text with their own *Minority Greek Text*.
The *motives* of men who handle the Word of God are most
important—especially, when they have taken the "scholarly"
world practically by storm since their 1881 Greek New Testament was published both in Greek, and in the E.R.V. form.
If they believed doctrines which the Bible does not teach,
and hence if they have held *heresies* in their theology, then
their *motives* must be taken into consideration. Westcott and

Hort threw out over ninety-nine percent (over fifty-two hundred) of the extant Greek manuscripts and evidence for the Greek New Testament in favor of retaining less than one percent (about forty-five manuscripts) of that extant evidence. They had a major stress on two manuscripts, the Vatican ("B") and the Sinai ("Aleph"). Whenever these two are in conflict, as they are in over three thousand places in the Gospels alone, Westcott and Hort always exalted the Vatican ("B"). This has been documented in Herman Hoskier's *Codex B and Its Allies*.

Though it is impossible to examine *motives* in a definitive manner, one thing is certain: if a man is a *heretic* in his views of theology, he is not particularly interested in handing a Bible-believing theological *fundamentalist* a Bible that backs up that fundamentalist theology. In fact, he is not even interested in promulgating a text which is the closest to the original autographs. He doesn't really care about the *exact wording, spelling, and phrasing of the Bible*, because he denies that the Bible was *verbally inspired* and *inerrant and infallible* in the original writings. A man's theology determines how he deals with God's Word.

C. Westcott and Hort's heresies contrast with John Burgon's soundness. There is a marked contrast with the theological *heresies* of Westcott and Hort and the theological soundness of Dean John William Burgon—the great Anglican author, scholar, and champion of the Traditional Text, or Received Text, and opponent of the phony Westcott and Hort text of the Greek New Testament. A picture of Dean Burgon, a conservative Anglican minister, is found on page 4 with the dates of his life. By way of contrast, the pictures of Bishop Westcott and Professor Hort, two liberal Anglican ministers, are found on page 6.

D. The quotations from *Which Bible?* which first prom-

posed this search for the heresies of Westcott and Hort. The book which first caused me to think about the theological *heresies* of *Westcott* and *Hort* was *Which Bible?* It is now in the fifth edition, 350 pages, indexed. I first read this in the first edition of 1970. Some of the major *heresies* were quoted by me in my article, "In Defense of the New Testament Majority Greek Text." In that pamphlet reprint, I wrote:

2. Views of Westcott and Hort, Defenders of the Minority Text. By way of contrast, however, the chief historical defenders of the Minority Text were B. F. Westcott and F. J. A. Hort (2,a, (1), p. 173). Though also Anglicans like Burgon, living around the same time as he, they held a *far inferior view of the Bible* and its doctrines. The *erroneous views* affected adversely their entire outlook on textual criticism of the Bible.

a. Westcott's Views. Westcott denied the historicity of Genesis 1 to 3. He wrote to the Archbishop of Canterbury, March 4, 1890: "No one now, I suppose, holds that the first three chapters of Genesis, for example, give a literal history—I could never understand how any one reading them with open eyes could think they did" (2,b, (1), 1st ed., p. 191). According to Benjamin Wilkinson, Westcott (as well as Hort) denied the substitutionary atonement of Christ. He wrote:

"Both rejected the atonement of the substitution of Christ for the sinner, or vicarious atonement; both denied that the death of Christ counted for anything as an atoning factor. They emphasized atonement through Incarnation" (2,b(1), 1st ed. p. 192).

b. Hort's Views. Hort, for example, concurred with Charles Darwin's false evolutionary theory. He wrote on April 3, 1860, "But the book which has most engaged me is

Darwin. Whatever may be thought of it, it is a book that one is proud to be contemporary with. . . . My feeling is strong that the theory is unanswerable" (2,b,(1), 1st ed., p. 189). Hort denied a literal Eden and a real Fall of man. He wrote:

"I am inclined to think that no such state as 'Eden' (I mean the popular notion) ever existed, and that Adam's fall in no degree differed from the fall of each of his descendants, as Coleridge justly argues" (2,b,(1), 1st ed., p. 191).

Hort called Christ's substitutionary atonement "immoral." Writing to Westcott, he said:

"I entirely agree—correcting one word—with what you there say on the atonement, having for many years believed that 'the absolute union of the Christian (or rather, of man) with Christ Himself' is the spiritual truth of which the popular doctrine of substitution is an *immoral and material counterfeit*. . . . Certainly nothing could be more unscriptural than the modern limiting of Christ's bearing our sins and sufferings to His death; but indeed that is only one aspect of an almost universal *heresy*.'" (2,b,(1), 1st ed., p. 192). (*op. cit.*, pp. 8-9).

In brief form, then, we find that other writers concurred with my own thinking that Westcott and Hort were indeed believers in various *heresies*. Because of this evidence, I decided to look for further evidence of the *heresies of Westcott and Hort* from their own books (if I could find any in print).

E. The books by Westcott and Hort that were used in this study The following books were examined as the basis of this report.

1. Three books by Brooke Foss Westcott.

a. *The Gospel According to St. John: The Authorized Ver-*

sion with Introduction and Notes (Wm. B. Eerdmans Publishing Company, Grand Rapids, Michigan, 1881 originally, but 1975 reprint. 307 pages)

b. *The Epistle to the Hebrews: The Greek Text with Notes and Essays* (Wm. B. Eerdmans Publishing Company, Grand Rapids, Michigan, 1889 originally, but 1974 reprinted, 504 pp.)

c. *The Epistles of St. John: The Greek Text, with Notes and Addenda* (Wm. B. Eerdmans Publishing Company, Grand Rapids, Michigan, 1883 originally, but 1974 reprinted, 248 pp.)

2. Two books by Fenton John Anthony Hort

a. *The First Epistle of St. Peter 1:2–2:17: The Greek Text with Introductory Lecture, Commentary, and Additional Notes* (James & Klock Publishing Company, Minneapolis, Minnesota, 1898 originally, but 1976 reprinted. 188 pp.)

b. *The Apocalypse of St. John 1–3: The Greek Text with Introduction, Commentary, and Additional Notes* (James & Klock Publishing Company, Minneapolis, Minnesota, 1908 originally, but 1976 reprinted. 47 pp.)

3. Short references to these five books for space-saving

To save space in this report, I'll use the following abbreviations for references to these five volumes:

a. Westcott's *Gospel of John* = "Westcott—*John*"
b. Westcott's *Hebrews* = "Westcott—*Hebrews*"
c. Westcott's *1, 2, & 3 John* = "Westcott—*1–3 John*"
d. Hort's *1 Peter* = "Hort—*1 Peter*"
e. Hort's *Revelation* = "Hort—*Revelation*"

F. Plan of treatment in this study will be by theological categories and headings. Rather than taking up each man or each book, I've chosen instead to take up the traditional and usual *theological divisions* and comment on the various *heresies* or *deviations from truth* that either of the two men have made in any of these divisions. The outline will therefore be the divisions as follows:

1. Bibliology
2. Theology Proper
3. Anthropology and Hamartiology
4. Demonology (or Satanology)
5. Ecclesiology
6. Pneumatology
7. Eschatology
8. Soteriology
9. Christology

Some of these theological headings have more under them than others, because of the various comments made by *Westcott* or *Hort* on these themes in their five books which have been analyzed. The comments will be as brief as possible, yet they will be clear.

G. What will be included in this theological analysis? There will be out-and-out *heresies* mentioned; there will be serious omissions of truth that should have been taught in a given verse, but were not; and there will be obscure things which are said without clarity by either *Westcott* or *Hort* so as to put a question mark as to where these men stand on vital issues in the Christian faith.

Chapter II

Heresies in Bibliology

In this general division of *Bibliography* there is usually taken up the doctrine of the Bible, including its inspiration, supernatural origin, canonicity, and the like [Cf. Lewis Sperry Chafer, *Systematic Theology*, 8 vols., Volume I]. Under this heading for *Westcott and Hort* I noted the following items, in varying degrees of *heresy* and/or *error*.

Vague or Erroneous Position on Inspiration, Revelation, or Inerrancy

1. Westcott wrongly claimed the "messengers" were "inspired" rather than only their *words*.

> (Hebrews 1:2) in the prophets . . . In whatever way God made Himself known to them, they were His messengers, *inspired* by His Spirit, not in their words only but as men. . . .
> —Westcott—*Hebrews, op. cit.*, p. 6

This is a *heresy* which many have accepted even in our

own day. Second Timothy 3:16–17, however, is very clear to refer that which is "God-breathed" or *"inspired of God"* only to the *"all scripture,"* or that which has been written down in words. The *men* were *not* "inspired" according to the Bible's clear statement here, only their *words* were *"inspired of God,"* or *"God-breathed."* Second Peter 1:20–21 tells us that the "holy men of God" spoke as they were *"moved by the Holy Spirit."* This *"moving"* or being *"borne along"* by the Holy Spirit is the correct way of speaking of God's use of His *men* in the writing of Scripture. If indeed the *men* were *"inspired,"* they would have been so throughout all their lives and in every situation, and hence would be *infallible* in all their utterances, written or spoken. Such was *not* the case, and this is nowhere taught in Scripture. *Inspiration* must refer only to the *words* of the Scripture as Second Timothy 3:16–17 clearly teaches. To go beyond the Bible at this point is laden with grave theological dangers.

2. Westcott implied that you could find *"revelation"* in *"Scripture,"* rather than equating *"revelation"* and *"Scripture."*

> (John 5:39-40). From the essential elements of revelation, external (voice, shape) and internal (word), the Lord passes to the record of *revelation in Scripture.*
>
> —Westcott—*John, op. cit.,* pp. 90-91

When you say there is a record of *"revelation in Scripture,"* you are implying that *some* of the Scripture might *not* contain *"revelation,"* but in certain portions of the *"Scripture,"* *there is some "revelation."* The proper teaching of the Bible on this matter is that *all* Scripture is God's *"revelation,"* and not just some parts of it. It was *all* *"revealed"* by God's Holy Spirit through the human writers. Again, this is an error which persists among the *liberals, modernists,* and *neo-orthodox* even to this day.

3. Hort seems to imply that *"all things necessary to salvation"* are the only really important things in the *"Scriptures."*

> So only, we believed, could the *unique character* of the Scriptures be rightly appreciated as "containing all things *necessary to salvation."*
>
> —Hort—*1 Peter, op. cit.,* p. vii

There is a thought here, as in modern times, to limit the *"Scriptures"* only to the *"all things necessary to salvation,"* implying that, perhaps, the historical, the geographical, the chronological, or the scientific matters, were either not important, or perhaps not given *inerrantly* or were not trustworthy. Men today who deny biblical *inerrancy* and *infallibility* in *all* matters of which they speak, limit these terms to things pertaining to *"salvation."* It could be a similar reference in Hort as well.

4. Hort omits any mention of verbal, plenary inspiration, or biblical inerraney or infallibility, and so does Westcott. Throughout the five books examined, both Westcott and Hort alike omit any stand for belief in a verbal, plenary inspiration of the Bible which also gives inerrancy and infallibility to the original writings. There is therefore a weak and *heretical* and unsatisfactory view of the Bible which is held by them. Often things which are *omitted* are more important an indication of a man's *heresies* than what he states in plain English. Learn to listen for "the absent note." For example, Hort, in commenting on First Peter 1:23, which states: "Being born again, not of corruptible seed, but of incorruptible, *by the word of God,* which liveth and abideth for ever," has this to say:

It [that is, the word translated *"Word"*] is God's whole
utterance of Himself in His incarnate Son, the *written or
spoken* record of this utterance or of any part of it being a
word only in a *secondary sense.*

—Hort—*1 Peter, op. cit.*, p. 93

This is a verse which has consistently been interpreted in
the past and in the present as a reference to the *"Word of
God"* being the Bible. Here, Hort comes along and states that
it is possibly a *"word only in a secondary sense."* This is a sort
of spiritualization of the "Word," rather than an acceptance
of it as the literal Bible which God produced through His
verbal, plenary inspiration.

**5. Westcott isolated belief *"in Christ"* from any *"proposi-
tions about Christ."*** In commenting about John 14:1, Westcott wrote:

The belief is "in Christ," and *not in any propositions
about Christ.*

—Westcott—*John, op. cit.*, p. 200

If you are not willing to place the meaning of *"belief in
Christ"* into the definite *"propositions about Christ"* as given
to us in the Bible, you have a *liberalistic* theology indeed. We
will see more of this under the all-important, definitive chapter below on *Christology.*

False or Erroneous Position on Biblical
Interpretation Principles

**1. Westcott referred to the historical *"Cain"* as only a *"typ-
ical example"* and as merely a *"representative"* rather than
being a historical person.** He wrote:

> (1 John 3:12) But the insertion of v. 11, the positive rule of Christians, leads to the insertion of the negative before the *typical example* of the opposite character. . . . The history of the first death naturally attracted wide attention as presenting in a *representative* and impressive *form* the issues of selfishness, self-will, sin.
>
> —Westcott—*1–3 John, op. cit.*, p. 110

This certainly does not sound like Westcott believed Cain was a genuine and real person. A *"representative form"* is *not* a real personage of history.

2. Hort denied that Paul actually saw the Lord Jesus Christ in an *outer vision*, stating that it was only an *"inner vision."*

> That is, (Revelation 1:1) Paul speaks of God as enabling him to have an *inner vision* and perception of His Son. . . .
>
> —Hort—*Revelation, op. cit.*, p. 3

This is a *heresy* clearly, since Acts 9 is so plain in pointing out that Paul saw a light brighter than the sun, and heard a voice. The men with him saw the light, and heard a sound, but couldn't understand what was being said. It was *outer,* and *not "inner."* A mere *"inner vision"* could not have *blinded* Paul.

3. Hort denies that the Book of *Revelation* is a *"repetition of words spoken by Christ to John,"* saying they are John's words in *"the prophetic spirit."*

> These epistles (Revelation 2:7) are *not merely a repetition a words spoken by Christ to John* in vision, but in speaking them he is moved by the *prophetic spirit.*
>
> —Hort—*Revelation, op. cit.*, p. 23

As a *"Revelation of Jesus Christ"* (Rev. 1:1), the entire book of *Revelation* is just that. It is not John's *"prophetic spirit"* at all, but the *Revelation* of Jesus Christ Himself.

4. Hort denies that *"Christ"* is the *"primary Revealer,"* thinking that it is *"God."*

> (Revelation 1:1) The conception of the book is *not* that the *primary Revealer is Christ,* though by the will or permission of God . . . ; but that the primary *Revealer is God.* . . .
> —Hort—*Revelation, op. cit.,* p. 5

Well, Christ is also *"God"* that is, He is *Deity.* Saying it this way almost denies the *deity* of Christ. It would appear that the expression, *"the revelation of Jesus Christ"* would indicate that the Lord Jesus *was* the *"primary Revealer."* John 16:12–15 clearly indicates that the Lord Jesus Christ Himself "has yet many things to say unto you, but ye cannot bear them now. Howbeit when he, the Spirit of truth, is come, he will guide you into all truth; for he shall not speak of himself; but whatsoever he shall hear, that shall he speak." The Book of *Revelation* is a part of the "many things" that Jesus Christ Himself had to say to His own.

False or Erroneous Position in Mixing Israel with the Church

1. Westcott erroneously called Israel of the Old Testament the *"old church."*

> The Christian Church (John 1:12) was not, as it might have been, the corporate transfiguration of the *old church,* but was built up of individuals . . . gives prominence to the act of personal faith which distinguishes the first-fruits of the *new Israel.*
> —Westcott—*John, op. cit.,* p. 8

The Church is a New Testament institution, and is *not* the *"new Israel,"* nor is the nation Israel in the Old Testament the *"old church."*

> (John 5:36) The *new church* grew out of the *old church*, as its proper consummation.
>> —Westcott—*John, op. cit.*, p. 24; for similar references, see also Westcott—*John*, p. 43, and Westcott-*Hebrews*, p. 51

2. Hort also erroneously looked at the *"Christian Church"* as the *"true Israel."*

> . . . nor is it less characteristic that he dwells on the significance of the conception of the *Christian church* as the *true Israel* by which all the Apostles were united (pp. 7, 16, 116).
>> —Hort—*1 Peter, op. cit.*, p. xii

> (1 Peter 2:9) It is less easy to see in what sense St. Peter termed the *new Israel* a royal priesthood.
>> —Hort—*1 Peter*, op. tit., p. 126

"Israel" is *"Israel"* and will never change. The *"Church"* is the *"Church"* and that will never change either. Neither becomes the other.

False, Erroneous, Weak, or Incomplete
Exegesis of Vital Verses

1. John 1:12 not clear on salvation. Westcott does not give a clear exegesis of John 1:12, one of the most simple verses on salvation in all of John. (See Westcott—*John* 1:12, *op. cit.*, pp. 9–9).

2. Other verses which are falsely interpreted, erroneous, weak, or incomplete in exegesis. According to my expectations, the following are verses which Westcott or Hort failed to expound accurately or completely to my satisfaction (with page references):

1. John 1:29 (Westcott—*John*, p. 20)
2. John 6 (p. 113 ff.)
3. John 7:3 (p. 116)
4. John 6:33 (Westcott—*John*, p. 102)
5. John 8:21 (Westcott—*John*, p. 130)
6. John 10:9 (Westcott—*John*, p. 153)
7. John 10:10 (Westcott—*John*, p. 154)
8. John 10:11 (Westcott—*John*, p. 154)
9. John 10:15 (Westcott—*John*, p. 155)
10. John 10:17–18 (Westcott—*John*, p. 156)
11. John 10:28 (Westcott—*John*, p. 158)
12. John 10:30 (Westcott—*John*, p. 159)
13. John 10:33 (Westcott—*John*, p. 159)
14. John 11:51 (Westcott—*John*, p. 175)
15. John 19:30 (Westcott—*John*, p. 278)
16. John 20:30–31 (Westcott—*John*, 297)

In Westcott's book on *Hebrews*, the following are weak or defective:

1. Hebrews 4:12 (Westcott—*Heb.*, p. 101)
2. Hebrews 5:9 (Westcott—*Heb.*, p. 129)
3. Hebrews 13:8 (Westcott—*Heb.*, p. 435)

Westcott was also weak or erroneous on the following verses in his book on 1–3 John:

1. 1 John 1:1 (p. 7)
2. 1 John 1:2 (Westcott—*1–3 John* , p. 8)
3. 1 John 1:2 (Westcott—*1–3 John,* p. 10)
4. 1 John 2:9 (Westcott—*1–3 John,* p. 88)

These ideas are merely suggestive as to the various *heresies* and otherwise *weaknesses* of both Westcott and Hort in the area of *bibliology,* or the doctrine of the Bible. The greatest *heresies* grow out of their failure to believe and to teach clearly in any of their five books the fact that the Bible is *verbally* and *plenarily inspired of God,* and consequently *infallible* and *inerrant* in the original writings. Without this clear stand on God's Word, the Bible, *Westcott* and *Hort's* theological position is likely to be loaded with *heresies* of one sort or another. And such is the case.

Chapter III

Heresies in Theology Proper

In this general division of *theology proper*, there is usually taken up the Trinity, and the nature of God Himself [cf. *Systematic Theology*, by Lewis Sperry Chafer, 8 Volumes, 1948, Dallas Seminary Press, Dallas, Texas, Volume I]. I noted the following items, in various degrees of *heresy* and/or *error*.

Westcott Embraced the Heresy of the Universal "Fatherhood of God"

1. Westcott believed *"Fatherhood of God"* could be applied to *"humanity"* as a whole because of creation in the *"Divine image."*

(John 4:21) Very much of the exact force of St. John's record of the Lord's words appear to depend upon the different conceptions of the *two forms* under which the *Fatherhood of God* is described. God is spoken of as *"the Father"* and as "my Father." Generally it may be said that the *Former title* expresses the original relation of God to being and *specially to humanity*, in virtue of man's *creation in the Divine image*, and the latter more particularly the relation of the Father to the Son Incarnate, and so indirectly *to man* in virtue of the Incarnation.

—Westcott—*John, op. cit.*, pp. 79–80

The term *"Father"* cannot refer to *"humanity"* as a whole outside of faith in Jesus Christ. This is *heresy* of the first dimension. Does not Westcott understand clearly John 8:44, where Jesus Christ taught *two fatherhoods?* Likewise, the term, *"my Father"* cannot refer to *"man"* as a whole either, but only to one redeemed by faith in the Lord Jesus Christ. It is *not* in virtue of *"the Incarnation"* that men can call God *"my Father,"* but by virtue of the vicarious and substitutionary sacrifice of the Lord Jesus Christ on the Cross.

2. Westcott clearly stated the *heretical* doctrine of the *"universal Fatherhood"* of God in discussing John 10:29.

(John 10:29) The thought, which is concrete in v. 28, is here traced back to its most absolute form as resting on the essential power of God in His relation of *universal Fatherhood*.

—Westcott—*John, op. cit.*, p. 159

This, again, is pure *heresy* as taught by the Lord Jesus Christ in John 8:44. To accept the heresy of the *"universal Fatherhood"* of God, is to misunderstand the total plan of redemption that God wrought out through His Son, Jesus Christ.

Westcott Denied That Christ Made Known God, the Father, as "God," Stating Only That He Made Him Known as "The Father"

(John 1:18) The Son made God known *not primarily as God*, but as *the Father.*

—Westcott—*John, op. cit.*, p. 15

This is *heretical.* Had Westcott never understood Colossians 2:9? It states clearly concerning Christ: "For in him dwelleth all the *fulness of the Godhead bodily."*

Westcott Denies That God Had to be "Propitiated" in the Sense of "Propitiating God"

(1 John 2:2). They shew that the scriptural conception of is *not* that of appeasing one who is angry, with a personal feeling, against the offender; but of altering the character of that which from without occasions a necessary alienation, and interposes an inevitable obstacle to fellowship. Such phrases as *"propitiating God'* and . . . are *foreign to the language of the N.T.*

—Westcott—*1–3 John*, p. 87

This is in error. God was *"propitiated"* by the sacrifice of His Son at Calvary's Cross. Thus God is now "propitious." As Chafer clearly indicates, *propitiation* is toward God as to its direction. He is "satisfied" with the work of His Son on the Cross of Calvary for our redemption.

Chapter IV

Heresies in Anthropology and Hamartiology

In this general division of *anthropology* and *hamartiology*, there is usually taken up the teachings on the origin of man, the element of man's being, the fall, the doctrine of sin (*"hamartiology"*), imputed sin, the sin nature, and so on. [Cf. Chaffer, *Systematic Theology, op. cit.*, Vol. II.] In this area, I noted the following items, in various degrees of *heresy* and/ or *error*.

Westcott Taught That Men Could Be Divine in Some Way

(John 17:22) Viewed from another point of sight it is the revelation of the *divine in man* realized in and through Christ.

—Westcott—*John, op. cit.*, p. 246

(1 John 2:18) . . . while the lie of Antichrist was to teach "that *man is divine apart from God in Christ.*"

—Westcott—*l–3 John, op. cit.*, p. 70

The clear teaching of Westcott in both of these places is that either *"man is divine"* when it's the action of *"God in Christ,"* or else there is a *"divine in man."* This is pure *heresy.* The Bible speaks of the believer partaking of the *"divine nature"* (2 Peter 1:4), but this is a far cry from making man in any sense *"divine."* The use of the word *"divine"* by Westcott is important as he uses this same word to describe the *"divinity"* of Christ later. He evidently means that Christ was no more *"divine"* than man can become, or else that man can become as *"divine"* as Christ was.

Westcott Espoused "Evolution" in Various Ways

> (Hebrews 1:2) The universe may be regarded either in its actual constitution as a whole . . . or as an order which exists through time *developed in successive stages.* There are obvious reasons why the *latter mode* of representation should be adopted here.
>
> —Westcott—*Hebrews, op. cit.,* p. 8

Here is a denial of the *immediate* creation by God of the entire universe and a *heretical* teaching of the *"development"* of the universe *"in successive stages."*

> (Hebrews 7:10) Each man is at once an individual of a race and a new power in the *evolution of the race.*
>
> —Westcott—*Hebrews, op. cit.,* p. 179

Again, Westcott's preference for Darwinian *heresy* in the form of *evolution* is in evidence.

Westcott Had a Heretical Theory of Man's Sinfulness and Depravity, Believing in Man's Perfectability in Various Ways

1. Westcott thought *"Christians"* are in a *"true sense 'christs.'"*

> (1 John 2:20) *"Christians"* are themselves *in a true sense "christs,"* anointed ones. . . .
>
> —Westcott—*1–3 John* op. tit., p. 73

Let this be remembered when Westcott deals with Jesus Christ. This is *heresy*. What confusion is wrought by Westcott in this statement. It *demeans* the Lord Jesus Christ and His exalted position, and it *wrongly exalts* sinners saved by God's grace into a level that they do not now merit. One day, we shall be "like Him," but not while we're on this earth.

2. Westcott believed in the *heresy* that *"man"* in general is, by possessing a *"spirit,"* *"united to heaven."*

> (John 3:6) (flesh . . . spirit) The words describe the characteristic principles of two orders. They are not related to one another as *evil* and *good;* but as the two spheres of being with which *man* is connected. By the *"Spirit" our complex nature is united to heaven*, by the "flesh" to earth.
>
> —Westcott—*John, op. cit.*, p. 50

Westcott does not say *believers* are, by their spirit, *"united to heaven,"* but clearly states it is *"man"* in general by *"our complex nature."* This *heresy* takes a wrong view of man's anthropology and his sinful nature, and, in effect, is *universalism*, because if a man is *"united to heaven"* already, what else need he do to be *saved* and go to heaven?

3. Westcott makes other *heretical* statements about man's perfectability and goodness as well.

> (Hebrews 2:7-8a) In spite of his frailty *man recognizes his divine affinity.*
>
> —Westcott—*Hebrews, op. cit.*, p. 43

Man is totally *depraved* and has *no "divine affinity"* whatsoever before he is saved.

> (Hebrews 2:8) For man, as he is, *still retains the lineaments of the divine image* in which he was made. He is *still able to pronounce an authoritative moral judgment:* he is still able to recognize that which corresponds with the *nature of God.*
>
> —Westcott—*Hebrews, op. cit.,* p. 60

Through the fall of man, he is *totally depraved*, and has, in himself, apart from Divine grace through faith in the Lord Jesus Christ and salvation which this brings, none of these things predicated of him by Westcott.

> (Hebrews 5:7) We can indeed form no clear conception of *"immortal," "incorruptible"* flesh; but the phrase represents to us the continuance under new conditions of all that belongs to t*he perfection of our nat*ure.
>
> —Westcott—*Hebrews, op. cit.,* p. 125

We have no *"perfection of our nature,"* and certainly we are not, outside of our resurrected, glorified bodies, either *"immortal"* or *"incorruptible."*

> (1 John 3:23) Thus in the three cases the Sonship of Jesus Christ is regarded in relation to God as the Father, to God as God, and to God as perfectly satisfying the *divine ideal which man is able to form.*
>
> —Westcott—*1–3 John, op. cit.,* p. 136

Again, *"man"* in himself is *not able* to *"form"* the *"divine ideal."* This is *heresy.*

Hort Held a Heretical View of Man's Psychology, Disbelieving the Teaching of 1 Thessalonians 5:23, and Taking "Soul" to Mean Merely "Life"

1. Hort spurned the *truth* of man's psychological make-up as clearly taught in I Thessalonians 5:23.

> (1 Peter 2:11) It is by this time sufficiently recognized that the modern religious sense of the term *"soul,"* as the *highest element in man, is founded on a misunderstanding of the N.T.* . . . and it is *dangerous to build an absolute psychology on such passages as* 1 Thess. v. 23.
>
> —Hort—*1 Peter*, op. cat., p. 134

Tell me, please, just why it is *"DANGEROUS"* to build an *"absolute psychology"* on the clear teachings of First Thessalonians 5:23 to the effect that the Christians in Thessalonica had spirits, souls, and bodies? If it is taught in the Word of God, we can use it to *"build"* on, regardless of what it is, so long as it is correctly interpreted in accordance with sound hermeneutical principles.

2. Hort confused *"soul"* with mere *"life,"* thus taking the *"soul"* as, in reality, part of the *material* part of man rather than the *immaterial*.

> (1 Peter 1:5) "salvation of souls". . . In these and similar phrases we must beware of importing into "soteria" the modern associations connected with the *religious use of the word "soul."* The *"soul"* in the bible *is simply the life* and *"to save a soul"* is the *opposite of "to kill."* . . .
>
> —Hort—*1 Peter*, op. cat., pp. 38–39

This is completely *false* and *erroneous* and *heretical* view of the *"soul"* in the Bible. "He that winneth *souls* is wise" certainly does *not* mean, he that "doesn't *kill people* is wise."

> (1 Peter 1:9) (salvation of souls) Here again, as I had occasion to say of v. 5, we have to be on our guard against interpreting the language of Scripture by the sharp limitations of modern usage. Salvation is deliverance from dangers and enemies and above all from death and destruction. The *soul is not a particular element or faculty of our nature, but its very life*
>
> —Cf. Westcott—of John xii. 25

First Thessalonians 5:23 clearly says that the *"soul"* as well as the *"spirit"* and the *"body"* are *"particular elements or faculties of our natures"* and that's good enough for me.

Chapter V

Heresies in Satanology

In this general division of *demonology* or *Satanology*, *th*ere is usually taken up the teachings on Satan and his demons, and so on [cf. Chafer, *Systematic Theology*, Vol. II]. In this area, I noted the following items, in various degrees of *heresy* and/or *error*.

Westcott Failed to Affirm the Personality of the Devil, Calling Him Only a "Power"

(1 John 3:8) From the very beginning we see *a power* in action hostile to God. Between these two, as between light and darkness, there can be no middle term.
> —Westcott—*1–3 John, op. cit.*, p. 106

Westcott was commenting on the "devil" and called him a mere *"power."* This is a sad *heresy*.

Hort Likewise Refused to Affirm the Personality of Satan, Calling Him Merely "the Power of Evil"

(Revelation 2:13) ("the throne of Satan") . . . but the visible supremacy of the *power of evil,* inspiring to evil.

—Hort—*Revelation, op. cit.,* p. 27

Satan and the Devil is more than a mere *"power"* as Westcott and Hort both heretically refer to him. The Lord Jesus Christ, in the context of John 8:44, clearly spoke of the Devil and Satan as a *person,* and so did Paul and the rest of the New Testament writers.

Chapter VI
Heresies in Ecclesiology

In this general division of *ecclesiology*, there is usually taken up the teachings on the church universal and the local church, with its ordinances, and so on [cf. Chafer, *Systematic Theology*, Vol. IV]. I noted, in this area, the following items, in various degrees of *heresy* and/or *error*.

Westcott Confuses the "Body" of Christ as the Body of Believers with Christ's Literal "Body" While on Earth

(Hebrews 9:11) Under one aspect these are represented by the union of the redeemed and perfected hosts made one *in Christ as His body*. Through this *glorified church* answering to the *complete humanity which Christ assume*, God is made known and in and through this each believer comes nigh to God. *In this body*, as a spiritual Temple, *Christ ministers*.

—Westcott—*Hebrews, op. cit.*, p. 258

There is not a clear enough distinction between the *"body*

of Christ" as the *true church*, or group of saved, born-again believers in Christ, and between the *"literal body of Christ"* which He had on earth, and now has in His glorified state in heaven. It tends to *de-emphasize* the truth that we have in the glory, the *"Man, Christ Jesus"* (1 Timothy 2:5), Who has a *body* which was *bodily resurrected* from the dead. It is a very confusing and erroneous doctrine of religious apostates today to stress the *"body of Christ"* meaning their heretical religious groups of adherents, and by so much, *deny* that Jesus Christ was *bodily raised from the dead,* and that He is *bodily now appearing in the presence of God the Father* for the believers in Him.

Westcott Believed the Heresy that the Church Ordinance of Water Baptism Was "the Condition of Regeneration"

(1 John 5:6) . . . and by His Baptism Christ fulfiled for the humanity which He took to Himself, though not for Himself, *the condition of regeneration.*

—Westcott—*1–3 John, op. cit.,* p. 181

This is more *heresy.* Since when is *"water baptism"* the *"condition of regeneration"*? It is by the grace of God, through personal *faith* in the Lord Jesus Christ. That is the *only* condition of regeneration known in Scripture (Ephesians 2:8–10).

Chapter VII

Heresies in Pneumatology

In this general division of *pneumatology*, there is usually taken up the teachings about God the Holy Spirit, including His Person, His Works, His Deity, and so on [cf. Chafer, *Systematic Theology*, Vol. VI]. In this area, I noted the following items, in various degrees of *heresy* and/or *error.*

Westcott Had a False View of Christ's Realization of "the Spirit" Within Him Beginning Only at His Baptism

> (John 1:33-34) At the same time we cannot but believe (so far as we realize the perfect humanity of Christ) that Christ at this *crisis first became conscious as man of a power of the Spirit within Him* corresponding to the new form of His work.
>
> —Westcott—*John, op. cit.*, p. 23

There is not a syllable of scriptural proof for this *heretical* statement. There is no reason whatsoever for assuming anything but that from the very moment of the Lord Jesus Christ's conscious awareness as the God-Man, He was fully aware of the power of God the Holy Spirit within Him. In Luke 2:49b, the Lord Jesus—*fully conscious* of Who He was and of God the Holy Spirit's *power* within Him—told his mother: ". . . wist ye not that I must be about my Father's business?"

Westcott Failed to Realize That God the Holy Spirit Dwelled Within the Believer, Despite the Clear Context Pointing to This Meaning

> (1 John 4:4) he that is in you, that is in the *Christian society*. . . . The Divine Person is *undefined*. We think naturally of God in Christ.
>
> —Westcott—*1–3 John, op. cit.*, p. 144

There should be no question but that the reference is to God the Holy Spirit, since the context of First John 4:1–4, there is repeated reference to various "spirits." The Greek relative pronoun, o{, [*ho*, "who or which"], is in the neuter, and is used in the context several times, referring to the word in Greek "spirit" which is also a neuter word. God the Holy Spirit would be the reference as in First Corinthians 6:19–20.

Hort Mistook a Reference to God the Holy Spirit for Merely "a Holy Spirit"

> (1 Peter 1:12) (by a holy spirit sent from heaven) . . .
>
> —Hort—*1 Peter, op. cit.*, p. 60

This clearly is a reference to *"the" Holy Spirit*, and *not "a" holy spirit*. Hort, in the context of his explanation, makes clear that this is *not* a reference to God the Holy Spirit, but to some human spirits. This is an error.

Chapter VIII

Heresies in Eschatology

In this general division of *eschatology*, there is usually taken up the teachings on prophecy, judgments, the eternal state, and so on [cf. Chafer, *Systematic Theology*, Vol. IV]. In this area, I noted the following items, in various degrees of *heresy* and/or *error.*

Westcott and Hort Held to Various Hereseis Concerning Eternal Life, Heaven, and the Eternal State

1. *"Heaven"* denied as a *"Place,"* but only spoken of as a *"state."*

> (John 1:18) The "bosom of the Father" *(like heaven) is a state and not a place.*
> —Westcott—*John, op. cit.*, p. 15

This is *heresy,* and the very opposite of the Lord Jesus Christ's clear teachings in John 14:1–3 where He speaks of going to prepare a *"place"* for us.

2. "Heaven" called the *"region of absolute and eternal truth."*

> (John 3:13) hath ascended up (gone up) to heaven . . .
> No man hath risen into *the region of absolute and eternal
> truth,* so as to look upon it face to face, and in the posses-
> sion of that knowledge declare it to men. . . .
>
> —Westcott—*John, op. cit.,* p. 53

Again, this is spiritualization of *heaven,* and is heretical.

**3. *"Heaven"* is made to be devoid of any *"local limita-
tion,"* but only symbolical of that which is *"spiritual."*** Westcott wrote:

> (John 14:2) (In my Father's house) . . . so it is to be
> conceived of the heavenly, as far as earthly figures can *sym-
> bolize* that which is spiritual. . . . But it is impossible to
> define further what is thus *shadowed out. Heaven* is where
> God is seen as our Father. We dare *not add any local limita-
> tion,* even in thought, to this final conception.
>
> —Westcott—*John, op. cit.,* p. 200

Again, this is *heresy.* Heaven *is* a *prepared "place"* as John
14:1–3 clearly states.

**4. *"Heaven"* seen as the *"hope"* of *"Assimilation of the
believer to his Lord."*** Westcott wrote:

> (1 John 3:3) And every one that hath this hope in Him.
> The practical conclusion from the great Christian *hope of
> the assimilation of the believer to his Lord* is given as a co-
> ordinate thought. . . .
>
> Westcott—*1-3 John, op. cit.,* p. 100

This is more heresy. The Christian will never be *"assimi-lated . . . to his Lord"* in the sense of becoming *"God"* or even part of God. The Christian who is saved, on the other hand, will be made *"like Christ"* and be "conformed to the image of His Son." The *"assimilation"* concept is like Nirvana or something else, and is *not* biblical.

5. *"Heaven"* again seen as *"figurative only"* regarding any *"local language."* Hort wrote:

> (1 Peter 1:5) (reserved in heaven) It is hardly necessary to say that this *whole local language is figurative only.* . . .
> —Hort—*1 Peter, op. cit.*, p. 37

More Hortian *heresy.*

Westcott Holds a False View of "Eternal Life," Seeing It as Present Only, and Not Going on Into the Future Eternity

> (John 5:24) (hath eternal life) He who knows the Gospel and knows that the Gospel is true cannot but have life. *eternal life is not future, but present.* . . .
> —Westcott—*John,* op cit., p. 87

The truth is that *eternal life* is both *present* for the believer and *future* as well.

> (1 John 3:14) "to enter into Life" . . . in this largest sense "life". . . is the fulfillment of the *highest idea of being: perfect truth in perfect action.*
> —Westcott—*1–3 John, op. cit.*, p. 112

This also is *heresy.*

(1 John 5:20) Eternal life is the *never-ending effort after this knowledge of God.*

—Westcott—*1–3 John, op. cit.*, p. 196

(1 John 5:20) The *"life eternal" is essentially present,* so far as it is the potential fulfillment of the idea of humanity.

—Westcott—*1–3 John, op. cit.*, p. 217

More heresy. Eternal life is the never-ending bliss of those who believe on the Lord Jesus Christ as their Savior which begins upon that faith, and never ends throughout all eternity future.

Hort Spiritualizes the "Second Death" or "Hell" into a Combination of the Deluge and Sodom"

(Revelation 2:11) (the second death) Then as to the order of promises, the *second death* stands between the Garden of Eden and the Manna. It might thus be *either the deluge,* as Bishop Temple implies, well called the *second death* in contrast to the expulsion from the Garden. It probably is a *combination of the deluge and Sodom,* the Waterflood and the Fire-Flood.

—Hort—*Revelation, op. cit.*, p. 27

This is false in the extreme, and constitutes a spiritualization of *hell* and the *lake of fire* which is the *"second death"* in Scripture.

Westcott Taught the Heresy of the Post-Millennial Return of Jesus Christ

(Hebrews 10: 13) The *return of Christ* appears to be

placed *after the conquestion of His enemies.* Compare 1 Corinthians 15:22 ff.

—Westcott—Hebrews, op. cit., p. 315

How about the *"Rapture"* of the living believers *before* the Tribulation? The Bible teaches clearly a *pre-millennial* coming of the Lord Jesus Christ, and *not* a *post-millennial* return.

Hort Denies the Literal Second Coming or "Revelation" of the Lord Jesus Christ

(1 Peter 1:7) (at the revelation of Jesus Christ) There is nothing in either this passage or others on the same subject, apart from the *figurative language of Thess.,* to show that the *Revelation* here spoken of is to be *limited to a sudden preternatural theophany. It may be a long and varying process,* though ending in a climax.

—Hort—1 Peter, pp. 44–45

Thessalonians does *not* have *"figurative language"* when speaking of the Second Coming of the Lord Jesus Christ. The *"revelation"* or "unveiling" of Christ will be *sudden,* and *not* a *"process."* This is *heretical.*

Chapter IX
Heresies in Soteriology

In this general division of *soteriology*, there is usually taken up the subjects of the doctrines about salvation, and similar topics [cf. Chafer, *Systematic Theology*, Vol. III]. In this area, I noted the following items, in various degrees of *heresy* and/or *error*.

Westcott Holds to the Heresy That the "Redemptive Efficacy of Christ's Work" Was to Be Found "in His Whole Life" Rather Than in His Death

(John 1:29) (which taketh away the sin of the world) The parallel passage in the Epistle (l.c.) shews that the *redemptive efficacy of Christ's work* is to be found *in His whole life* (He was manifested) crowned by His Death.
—Westcott—*John, op. cit.*, p. 20

The Bible is silent as to *"His whole life"* as forming any basis whatever for *"the redemptive efficacy of Christ's work."* It was as the *"Lamb of God"* that He could "take away the sin of the world" (John 1:29), and this *"Lamb"* was crucified and shed His precious blood (1 Peter 1:18–19) as the atonement and sacrifice for the sins of the whole world. "Without the shedding of blood is no remission" (Hebrews 9:22). To say that Christ's *"whole life"* had anything to do with the *"redemptive efficacy of Christ's work"* is to partake of the *heresy* of modernistic religious *apostasy*.

Westcott Makes a Series of Statements That Teach the Heresy of "Universalism" in Salvation, Either Clearly, or by Implication

(John 3:12) Such was the full revelation of the Son, involving the redemption of the *world* and the *reunion of man with God*, which is indicated in the three following verses.

—Westcott—*John, op. cit.*, p. 52

This seems to teach that *"man"* as such, including *all men*, is *"reunited with God"* automatically. This is *universalism*.

(John 10:16) (bring) This could only be by His death, *which reunites man with God. . . .*

—Westcott—*John, op. cit.*, p. 155

Again, this is the *heresy* of *universalism*.

(Hebrews 2:8-9) The fruit of His work is *universal*.

—Westcott—*Hebrews, op. cit.*, p. 44

Again, here is a possible reference to the false *heresy* of *universalism*. This could imply that *all men are saved* because of the "fruit of His work," and this is *false*:

(Hebrews 2:9) The glory which followed the death marked its *universal efficacy*. Thus Christ was made lower than angels that He might accomplish this *complete redemption*.

—Westcott—*Hebrews, op. cit.*, p. 46

This could imply that *everyone is redeemed automatically*, which is *universalism*.

(1 John 1:1) That which we understand by the eternal purpose of God (Eph. i.4), the relation of the Father to the Son (John xvii.5), *the acceptance of man in the beloved* (Eph. i.6), was already. . . .

—Westcott—*1–3 John, op. cit.*, p. 4

This is pure *heresy* and is *universalism*. *"Man"* as such, is *not "accepted in the beloved,"* but only those who are born-again by faith in Christ.

(1 John 1:2) "Additional Note On i. 2. *The Fatherhood of God."* The idea of the *divine Fatherhood*, answering to that of human sonship and childship (see Additional Note on iii. I), occupies an important place in the writings of St. John.

—Westcott—*1–3 John, op. cit.*, p. 27

This certainly sounds like the *heresy* of the *universal Fatherhood of God*, and the *universal brotherhood of man*.

(1 John l:7) . . . in Him *all men find their true life.*
—Westcott—*1–3 John, op. cit.*,p. 35

This could imply that *"all men"* find *"eternal life"* in Christ, which is false and is *heretical*. Only those who have *faith* in Christ find *"eternal life."*

> (1 John 2:2) Christ's *advocacy of man* is addressed to God in that relation of *Fatherhood* which has been fully revealed in the Son who has taken manhood to Himself.
> —Westcott—*1–3 John, op. cit.,* p. 43

But Christ was *not* the *"Advocate"* of *"man"* as such—including *all mankind*. He is only the *"Advocate"* for the believer. Nor is *every man* the partaker of God's *"Fatherhood,"* but only the believer in Christ.

> (1 John 2:12) *Forgiveness is granted to men* because Christ is indeed what He is revealed to be and what His "name" expresses.
> —Westcott—*1–3 John, op. cit.,* p. 59

This again is the *heresy* of *universalism*. *"Forgiveness"* is *not* *"granted to men"* of all sorts and of all kinds *universally,* but only to those who believe in Christ as their Savior.

> (1 John 2:18) The teaching of Antichrist leaves God and the world still ununited. The proclamation of the *union* is the *message of the Gospel.*
> —Westcott—*1–3 John, op. cit.,* p. 70

The *"message of the Gospel"* is *not* that there is now a *"union"* of *"the world"* with "God." There is only a *"union"* between God and the believer in Christ.

> (1 John 4:2-3) The Incarnate Savior is the *pledge of the complete redemption and perfection of man.* . . .
> —Westcott—*1–3 John, op. cit.* p. 140

The way this reads, the mere *"incarnation"* of Christ guar-
antees automatically the *"complete redemption and perfection
of man,"* which is *heresy* and *universalism.*

All of these above quotations tend to show very clearly
that Westcott was a believer in the *heresy* of *universalism* in
the area of salvation and redemption, thus believing that *all
men,* whether they trust Christ as Savior or not, are *saved*
and *redeemed,* and therefore possessors of *eternal life,* and
forgiveness of sins, and therefore are going to *heaven.* Nothing could be farther from the truth.

Westcott Has an Erroneous View of "Eternal Life."

**1. He thought a Christian never *"is"* but was *"always . . .
becoming.*** Westcott wrote:

> (John 15:8) (and so shall ye be [become] my disciple) A
> *Christian never "is," but always "is becoming" a Christian.*
> —Westcott—*John, op. cit.,* p. 219

This would mean that salvation was not a once-for-all
transaction as in the new birth of John 3, but merely a *process.* This is *heresy.* When a person is born again by simple
faith in Jesus Christ as Savior, he is a *"Christian"* and can
never be any more a *"Christian"* than when he was first *born*
a *Christian.* He can *grow* in the ways of the Christian faith,
but he is not any less a *Christian* any more than your child is
any less your child, whether at the moment of his birth, or at
the moment of his death.

2. He had a false and phony conception of *"eternal life."*
Westcott wrote:

> (1 John 3:14) "To enter into life". . . In this largest sense
> "life". . . . is the fulfillment of the *highest idea of being: per-*

fect in truth in perfect action.

—Westcott—*1–3 John* , *op. cit.* p. 112

This simply is *false* and foreign to the clear teachings of the Bible.

(1 John 5:20) *Eternal life* is the *never-ending effort after this knowledge of God.*

—Westcott—*1–3 John, op. cit.,* p. 196

This is pure *heresy.* *"Eternal life"* is under *no* circumstances an *"effort"* on the part of man. It is, on the contrary, the result of unmerited favor and grace of God through a man's personal faith in Christ.

(1 John 5:20) The *"life eternal"* is *essentially present,* so far as it is the potential fulfillment of the idea of humanity. . . .

—Westcott—*1–3 John, op. cit.,* p. 217

Wrong. So far as being "present," it is present, but the *"essential"* nature of it is unending and eternal, and hence *future* as well. *Both "present"* and *"future"* are present for the believer in Christ who possesses eternal life.

Chapter X

Heresies in Christology

In this general division of *Christology*, there is usually taken up the subjects of the Person and Work of Christ, and similar topics [cf. Chafer, *Systematic Theology*, Vol. V]. Under this area, I noted the following items, in various degrees of *heresy* and/or *error*. This is the most extensive area of *heresy* on the part of *Westcott* and *Hort*, and is also the most *important* area of *heresy*, since it relates both to the *Person* and to the *work* of the Lord Jesus Christ.

The Heresies of Westcott and Hort on the *Person* of the Lord Jesus Christ

A. *The elimination of or the denial of the eternal pre-existence of the Lord Jesus Christ*

1. Westcott objects to the *"pre-existence"* of Christ in John 1:1. He wrote:

> (John l: l) (In the beginning) The "being" of the Word is thus necessarily carried beyond the limits of time, *though*

the pre-existence of the Word is definitely not stated. The simple affirmation of existence in this connection suggests a loftier conception than that of *pre-existence;* which is embarrassed by the idea of time. . . .

—Westcott—*John, op. cit.,* p. 2

If the *"Word"* was "in the beginning" and with God, and was God, He most certainly would have to be *"pre-existent."* John 1:1 and following clearly teach this.

2. Westcott denied Christ's *"pre-existence"* in John 1:15. He wrote:

(John 1:15) He that cometh after me is preferred before me. The *supposed reference to the pre-existence of the Word . . . seems to be inconsistent* with the argument which points to a present consequence. . . .

—Westcott—*John, op. cit.,* p. 13

Only a *"supposed"* reference, says Westcott, to the *"pre-existence"* of the Word. "For he *was* before me" certainly implies His eternal *pre-existence.*

3. Westcott merely said that the words of John 17:24 *"imply"* the *"pre-existence"* of Christ, rather than *clearly teach this*. He wrote:

(John 17:24 (Before the foundation . . .) The words distinctly *imply* the *personal pre-existence of Christ.*

—Westcott—*John, op. cit.,* p. 248

These words do more than *"imply"* it, they specifically, and definitely *teach* the *"pre-existence"* of Christ. Otherwise, how could Christ have "glory" and how could the Father love Him *before the foundation of the world"?*

4. Westcott, with his questioning of the *"pre-existence"* of Christ, calls a *"strange opinion"* the thought that *"Melchizedek"* was a *"Christophany."* He wrote:

> (Hebrews 7:1) Two other *strange opinions* may be noticed. Some orthodox Christians supposed that *Melchizedek was an incarnation of the Son of God* or perhaps simply a *Christophany.*
>
> —Westcott—*Hebrews, op..cit.*, p. 202

This is not so *"strange"* as Westcott believes. I think that Melchizedek was a *theophany* or a *Christophany* judging from the language both of Genesis and of Hebrews.

B. *The questioning of the* omniscience *of the Lord Jesus Christ.*

In various places, Westcott questions or omits completely the *omniscience* of Christ. He wrote:

> (John 1:42) (Thou art) This is *not necessarily a prophetic declaration* by *Divine knowledge.*
>
> —Westcott—*John, op. cit.*, p. 25

Here is a down-playing of Christ's *omniscience.*

> (John 1:48) (when thou wast under the fig tree, I saw thee) . . . the Lord shewed His *Divine insight* into the heart of man.
>
> —Westcott—*John, op. cit.*, p. 27

This was more than *"insight,"* it was *"omniscience."*

> (John 11:11) (his glory) The manifestation of His glory in this "sign" must *not be sought* simply in what we call its

"miraculous" element, but in this taken in connection with the circumstances, as a revelation of the *insight*, the sympathy, the sovereignty of the Son of Man. . . .

—Westcott—*John, op. cit.*, p. 39

(John 2:24-25) (he knew what was in man) Only on rare occasions does He ask anything, as if all were not absolutely *clear before His eyes*. . . . But St. John exhibits this attribute of *complete human knowledge* most fully. . . . At other times it appears to be the *result of an insight* which came from a perfect spiritual sympathy, found in some degree among men. . . . A careful study of these passages seems to shew beyond doubt that the *knowledge of Christ . . . has its analogues in human powers*. His *knowledge* appears to be truly the *knowledge of the* Son of Man, and *not* merely the *knowledge of the Divine Word*, though at each moment and in each connection it was, in virtue of His perfect humanity, *relatively complete*.

—Westcott—*John, op. cit.*, p. 46

This is pure *heresy*. Christ's *"knowledge"* was *not* only *"relatively complete,"* but He knew *everything* as being *omniscient*. His *knowledge* had *no "analogues in human powers"* at all, but was the result of Deity and the attribute of Deity, namely, *omniscience*.

(John 4:1) (When therefore the Lord knew . . .) Nothing implies that the *knowledge* of the Lord was *supernatural* (see ii. 24, note).

—Westcott—*John, op. cit.*, p. 66

Again, here is a denial of His *omniscience*.

C. Westcott questions the omnipresence of the Lord Jesus Christ, making only "the Spirit" fulfilling this role.

> (John 14:16) (for ever) Christ's historical *presence was only for time.* His spiritual Presence was "for all the days until the consummation of the age" (Matt. xxviii. 20). *This presence was fulfilled through the Spirit.*
>
> —Westcott—*John, op. cit.,* p. 205

This is incorrect. The Lord Jesus Christ Himself is also *omnipresent,* and is here wherever believers are, the same as is God the Father and God the Holy Spirit.

D. Westcott and Hort deny or question the Deity of the Lord Jesus Christ

1. Westcott said the *"Word"* was *"distinct from 'God,'"* and only *"essentially 'God,'"* but not *"God"* actually. He wrote:

> (John 1:1) Because the *Word* was personally *distinct from "God"* and yet *essentially "God,"* He could make Him known.
>
> —Westcott—*John, op. cit.,* p. 2

If the Lord Jesus Christ was *"distinct from God,"* then He could not have been *"God."* John 1:1 affirms that He *"was God"* as the *Word,* and yet Westcott wants merely to say that He was *"essentially God"* without being *actually God.* This qualifying word, *"essentially,"* should not be used if Westcott wishes to affirm Christ's absolute *Deity.* Christ was *"God"* without any qualifications whatsoever, just like the Father was *"God"* and the Holy Spirit was *"God"* and they all *are* and *will* be *"God"* also into eternity future. Westcott wants to use the term *"God"* only for the Father. This is *heresy.*

> (John 1:1) (the Word was God) Thus we are led to conceive that the *Divine nature* is *essentially in the Son. . . .*
> —Westcott—*John, op. cit.,* p. 3

It is more than the *"Divine nature"* being *"essentially in the Son,"* but *Deity* was and is *actually in the Son. "Essentially"* is a limiting word which is not clear and is not needed if Westcott really wishes to affirm Christ's *Deity.* More than the *"Divine nature"* is in the *Son.* It is spoken of the believers that they might be "partakers of the *divine nature"* (1 Peter 1:4b), yet it is never spoken of believers that they are *Deity* or *God.* This is a weak term, when speaking of Christ.

2. Westcott falsely interprets *"all the fulness of the Godhead bodily"* merely to mean the *"sum of the Divine attributes."* He wrote:

> (John 1:16) St. Paul says that "all the fulness dwelt" in Christ (i. 19), and more definitely, that "all the *fulness of the Godhead* dwells in Him. . . ." Here St. Paul's thought is evidently that the *whole sum of the Divine attributes exists together in Christ,* and that each Christian in virtue of his fellowship with Him draws from that "fulness" whatever he needs for the accomplishment of his own part in the great life of the Church.
> —Westcott—*John, op. cit.,* p. 14

All the *"fulness of the Godhead bodily"* by all means *must* mean the clear fact that Jesus Christ was *"God"* and *"Deity."* To say it merely means that He had the *"sum of the Divine attributes"* does not clearly state or imply that He was and is *God* and *Deity.* An *"attribute"* of God is *not "being God."*

3. Westcott falsely interprets *"making himself equal with God"* to mean merely placing *"his action on the same level with the action of God."* He wrote:

> (John 5:18) He called God His own Father (Rom. viii. 32)— His Father in a peculiar sense—making Himself *equal with God*, by *placing His action on the same level with the action of God.*
>
> <div align="right">—Westcott—<i>John, op. cit.</i>, p. 84</div>

The Lord Jesus claimed to actually be *"God,"* and not simply to place *"His action"* on the *"same level with the action of God."* This falls far short of the true *Deity* of Christ, and is not acceptable.

4. Westcott falsely stated Christ was only *"in absolute union with God"* rather than actually *being God*. He wrote:

> (John 8:28) (that I am, and that I do nothing of myself) . . . perceive, that is, that my being alike and my action are raised above all that is limited, and in *absolute union with God*.
>
> <div align="right">—Westcott—<i>John, op. cit.</i>, p. 132</div>

If Christ's actions were *"in absolute union"* with *"God,"* then He couldn't be *God*, could He? *"God"* and Christ are different to Westcott, when in reality, Christ is *"God"* and *"Deity"* without qualification.

5. Westcott denied that the Lord Jesus Christ and God the Father could be *"equal in power,"* hence denied thereby the *Deity* of Christ. He wrote:

> (John 10:30) (I and my Father are one). It seems clear that the unity here spoken of cannot fall short of unity of

essence. The thought springs from the *equality of power* (my hand, the Father's hand); but infinite power is an essential *attribute of God;* and it is *impossible to suppose that two beings distinct in essence could be equal in power.*

—Westcott—*John, op. cit.,* p. 159

Westcott is vague here, but he seems to be saying that there could be no *"equality in power"* between God the Father and God the Son. If there is no *"equality in power,"* there can be no *Deity* of Christ, and Christ could not in fact be *"God."*

6. Westcott, by saying Jesus was only *"one with God,"* denied that He was *"God"* himself. He wrote:

(John 10:34) (Jesus answered . . .) This, they argued, was violated if Jesus, truly man, claimed to be *one with God.*

—Westcott—*John, op. cit.,* p. 160

You cannot be *"one with God"* and be *"God"* also. Thus, Westcott was denying that Jesus Christ was *"God."*

7. Westcott spoke of the *"special relation"* in which *"Christ stood to God"* for Martha, thus denying that *Christ* was in effect *"God"* Himself. He wrote:

(John 11:22) (I know) The emphatic repetition of God, at the end of both clauses in the original, serves to bring out, as it were, the *special relation in which Christ stood to God* in Martha's thoughts.

—Westcott—*John, op. cit.,* p. 168

If *"Christ"* merely *"stood"* in a *"special relation . . . to God,"* then He by no means could be considered by Westcott as *"God"* Himself.

8. Westcott denies that *"thy throne, O God,"* in Hebrews 1:8 refers to Christ's *Deity* or that this is even the proper translation. He wrote:

> o Qeo" can be taken as a *vocative* in both cases (Thy throne, O God, . . . therefore, O God. Thy God . . .) or it can be taken as the subject (or the predicate) in the first case (God is Thy throne, or Thy throne is God . . .), and in opposition to in the second case (Therefore God, even Thy God . . .). . . . Thus on the whole it seems best to adopt in the first clause the rendering: God is Thy throne (or, Thy throne is God). . . . It is commonly supposed that the force of the quotation lies in the *Divine title* (o Qeo") which, as it is held, is applied to the *Son*. It seems however from the whole form of the argument to lie *rather* in the description which is given to the Son's office and endowment.
>
> —Westcott—*Hebrews, op. cit.*, pp. 25–26

What Westcott is saying, in essence, is that the translation of the KJB, *"thy throne, O God,"* applying as it does, directly to the Lord Jesus Christ—though perfectly good Greek, and within the rules of Greek syntax, taking *"O God"* in the vocative case—is rejected completely by him, thus denying that this passage teaches clearly the *Deity* of Christ.

9. Hort denies that *"Lord"* In 1 Peter 1:3 refers to the *Deity* of Christ, but merely means *"teacher."* He wrote:

> (1 Peter 1:3) Blessed be the God and Father of our *Lord* Jesus Christ) In all this early usage probably represents *not* Adon, but the nearly equivalent Aramaic Mar, sometimes applied to *teachers by disciples.* . . .
>
> —Hort—*1 Peter, op. cit.*, p. 31

Thus, Hort re-defines *"Lord:"* to mean merely *"teacher"* instead of *"Lord"* and *Deity* as a title for the Lord Jesus Christ.

10. Hort shows that he does not consider the Lord Jesus Christ as *"God"* by his comment on Revelation 1:1. He wrote:

> (Revelation 1:1) The conception of the book is *not* that the primary Revealer is *Christ*, though by the will or permission of *God;* but that the primary Revealer is *God,* Christ being both that which is revealed and the supreme or immediate instrumental Revealer.
>
> —Hort—*Revelation, op. cit.,* p. 5

Hort here seems to be denying that *Christ* is *"God"* since he refers to Him in terms other than that term. He could have said that it was *"God the Father"* he believed to be the Revealer, rather than *"God the Son,"* and hence preserved the *Deity* of the Lord Jesus Christ without question.

11. Hort denied that Christ was *"God"* in Revelation 1:2 as well. He wrote:

> (Revelation 1:2) . . . John's conveyance of the revelation to the churches, just as he had received it from the angel, and the angel from Christ, *and Christ from God.*
>
> —Hort—*Revelation, op. cit.,* p. 7

If indeed *"Christ"* received something from *"God,"* then Hort did not consider Christ to be Himself *"God."*

12. Hort denied that the Lord Jesus Christ was spoken of as *"Alpha and Omega,"* and *"Lord God,"* and *"the Almighty."* He wrote:

> (Revelation 1:8) I am Alpha and Omega, the beginning and the ending, saith the Lord (God), which is, and which was, and which is to come, the Almighty) This verse must stand alone. The *speaker cannot be our Lord,* when we con-

sider 1.4 . . . and *all scriptural analogy is against the attri-
bution of* with or without *to Christ*

> —Hort—*Revelation, op. cit.*, p. 13

What Hort is saying is that *"Lord God"* cannot refer to the
Lord Jesus Christ, because that would clearly give His *Deity*,
and Hort does not believe that there are any *"scriptural anal-
ogies"* for this, much less for Christ to be called the *"Almighty."*
How about John 20:28, where Thomas declares that Jesus
Christ is *"my Lord and my God"*? This shows how Hort goes
to any length to *deny* the *Deity* of Christ or to say He is *"God."*
The word in Greek for *"God"* does not even appear in the text
of the Received Text on which the KJB is based, but the Westcott and Hort false text does contain the word *"God"* at this
point. Even so, Hort *rejects* this affirmation of the Lord Jesus
Christ, when it seems so clearly to apply to Him.

**13. Hort said the *"Arian meaning"* referring to Christ as
the *"first thing created"* just *"might"* be possible, thus denying His Deity.** He wrote:

> (Revelation 3:15) The words *might* no doubt bear *the
> Arian meaning "the first thing created"* . . .
> —Hort—*Revelation, op. cit.*, p. 36

Hort goes on to say these words "equally well bear" another sense, but the fact remains that Hort could even say
these words *"might no doubt bear the Arian meaning"* that the
Lord Jesus Christ was *"the first thing created,"* really means
that Christ could not have been *God* or *Deity*, since He was
but a *created being* of God. This is the purest of *heresies* on the
Person of Christ.

**14. Westcott sidesteps Thomas's clear affirmation that
Jesus Christ was *"God,"* and claims Christ never spoke of
Himself directly *"as God."*** He wrote:

(John 20:28) And Thomas answered and said unto him, My Lord and *my God*) . . . and the words which follow shew that the Lord accepted the declaration of *His Divinity* as the *true expression of faith. He never speaks of Himself directly as God* (comp. v. 18), but the aim of His revelation was to lead men to *see God in Him.*

—Westcott—John op. cit., p. 297

Here Thomas had given Christ the most resounding and clear denomination of *Deity* and had named Him as *"God,"* and yet Westcott lowers the terms merely to *"divinity"* and then merely said of this lower term [Westcott and other clever modernist apostates have a different meaning of *"divinity"* than we do of the word *"Deity"* of *"God"* and affirm that *man* himself also has *"divinity"* with variations as to whether this *"divinity"* is but a little *"spark"* or a full *"flame"*] that it is a *"true expression of faith."* What about its being a *"fact"*? This he does not say. It reminds me of Bishop Pike (the late Anglican bishop in America) who said he didn't believe the Creed, but he could *sing* it, and explain it away thereby. When the Lord Jesus Christ said, *"Before Abraham was, I AM,"* the Jews knew He was *"speaking of himself directly as God,"* and they took up stones to stone Him (John 8:58–59). He said again *"I and my Father are one,"* and again the Jews took up stones to stone Him because they understood clearly that He was *"making himself God"* (John 10:30–33). Westcott and Hort both have shown themselves to *deny* the full and clear *Deity* of Christ and go all around the point to keep from admitting clearly that the Lord Jesus Christ was, is, and ever will be *God the Almighty Son.* What *heresy.*

E. Westcott questions or denies the impeccability or sinlessness *of the Lord Jesus Christ*

　　1. Westcott seemed to imply that the Lord Jesus Christ

had *sin* just like *"every individual in the whole race."* He wrote:

> (John 1:51) *All* that *truly belongs to humanity, all* therefore that *truly belongs to every individual in the whole race, belongs also to Him.*
>
> —Westcott—*John, op. cit.,* p. 35

This statement would indicate that Westcott wrongly thought that *sin* also belonged to the Lord Jesus Christ, since *sin "truly belongs to every individual in the whole race."* This is a denial of the *impeccability* and *sinlessness* of Christ.

2. Westcott wrongly thought Christ's *"perfection"* was not reached *"till after death,"* and therefore denies His *sinlessness*. He wrote:

> (Hebrews 2: 10) The conception of it is that of bringing Christ to the *full moral perfection of His humanity* (cf. Luke xiii. 32), which carries with it the completeness of *power and dignity. . . .* This *"perfection" was not reached till after death. . . .*
>
> —Westcott—*Hebrews, op. cit.,* p. 49

If indeed the Lord Jesus Christ did not reach this *"perfection"* until *"after death,"* this would mean that He was *imperfect* and therefore *sinful* throughout His earthly life. Such is the gravest of *heresies.* He was *perfect* and *sinless* and *impeccable* from the moment of His birth in Bethlehem.

3. Westcott wrongly thought that Christ's *"perfection"* had to do with His *"earthly discipline."* He wrote:

> (1 John 3:3) (even as He (Christ) is pure) The result of the *perfection of His earthly discipline* (Heb. v. 7 ff.) still abides in His glorified state.
>
> —Westcott—*1–3 John, op. cit.,* p. 101

This appears to base the Lord Jesus Christ's *"perfection"* upon *"His earthly discipline,"* which would mean that without this *"discipline,"* He would be less that *perfect.* Such is contrary to the Bible, and constitutes a denial of the *sinlessness* and *impeccability* of the Lord Jesus Christ. He had a *perfect* and *sinless* human nature as well as a *perfect* and *sinless* nature of deity, as the *God-Man.*

F. Hort holds a heretical view of what is involved in Christ's messiahship

1. Hort falsely held that Old Testament prophets had "Christhood" and had "messiahship." He wrote:

> (1 Peter 1:11) "Touch not mine anointed ones **(Tw`n cristw`n mou`)** and do my prophets no harm," where the Divine anointing or *Christhood* and prophethood are set in parallelism as kindred attributes of the children of Israel. . . . The prophet, the people to whom he belongs and to whom he speaks, and the dimly seen Head and King of the people *all* pass insensibly one into the other in the language of prophecy; *they all are partakers of the Divine anointing, and the messiahship which is conferred by it.*
>
> —Hort—*1 Peter*, op. cit., p. 52

If this is true, then the Lord Jesus Christ did not have any unique *"messiahship"* at all, but was only one in a long line of *"messiahs."* This is a false view of the meaning of the Old Testament promised *"Messiah."*

2. Hort emphatically denied that the *"sufferings destined for Messiah"* were fulfilled in the *"sufferings of Christ"* when here on earth. He wrote:

(1 Peter l:11) (the sufferings destined for Messiah) *This cannot possibly mean the sufferings of Christ* in our sense of the words, i.e. the sufferings which as a matter of history *befell the historical Christ. . . .*

—Hort—*1 Peter, op. cit.,* p. 54

Here is a complete denial of the accuracy of prophetic utterance, and a misconception of the Word of God and of the sufferings of the Lord Jesus Christ as the *Messiah.* It is a denial of Peter's words as well.

G. Westcott and Hort are confused and in error on the proper teaching of the Person and natures of the Lord Jesus Christ.

1. Westcott denies the *"express affirmation"* by John that the *"Word"* was *"Jesus Christ."* He wrote:

(John 1:18) He does not *expressly affirm* but *assumes* the identification of the *Word with Jesus Christ* (v. 17).

—Westcott—*John, op. cit.,* p. 16

John 1: 14 most *clearly* and *"expressly affirms"* that "the *Word* became *flesh* and *dwelt* among us, and we beheld His glory, the glory as of the *only begotton of the Father."* What more *"express affirmation* could you need?

2. Westcott elevates the possibilities in a *"perfect human life"* of a regular human being, and then *lowers* the Lord Jesus Christ by applying this to Him. He wrote:

(John 2:2:3) *A perfect human life,* a life lived, that is, in *absolute harmony with the Divine,* will therefore in every point reveal to those who have the eyes to see, *something of*

God, of His "glory." *This beign so,* it is clear that all the acts and sufferings of "the *Son of Man*" were essentially revelations of glory. . . .

—Westcott—*John, op. cit.,* p. 46

Westcott's view of the true hypostatic union of God and Man in Christ is defective. Here he so exalts the human beings into making it possible to behold their lives and see *something of God,"* on the one hand, and on the other hand, he *demeans* the Lord Jesus Christ and *lowers* Him, by talking about Him in the same breath with sinful, frail man. He was *God* as well as perfect, sinless, holy *Man* in a sense that cannot even be compared with sinful, immoral, fallen man. He had a true humanity, this is true, but He is the *incomparable Christ.*

3. Westcott expressed amazement that Christ's work was *"co-ordinate with"* that of *"the Father,"* calling it *"remarkable."* He wrote:

(John 5:17) The form of the sentence is *remarkable.* Christ place *His work as co-ordinate with that of the Father,* and *not* as dependent on it.

—Westcott—*John, op. cit.,* p. 84

Why is it so *"remarkable,"* if, that is, you hold to Christ's absolute *Deity* and that He was *"very God of very God"* who was *co-equal* with God the Father and God the Holy Spirit in every attribute, barring none?

4. Westcott agree with *"elements"* in two *wild* interpretations of Christ's *"ascending up"* both of which violate the true *nature* of the Lord Jesus Christ. He wrote:

(John 6:62) What and if ye shall see the Son of man *ascend up* where he was before?) This incomplete question

. . . has been interpreted in *two* very different ways. . . . According to the *first interpretation* the *"ascending up"* is the Ascension as the *final spiritualizing of the Lord's person,* whereby the offence of the language as to His flesh would be removed by the apprehension of the truth as to His *spiritual humanity.* In the *second,* the *"ascending up"* is referred to the *"elevation" on the cross.* . . . *Each of these two interprations appears to contain elements of the full meaning.*

—Westcott—*John, op. cit.,* p. 109

This is pure *heresy* from two standpoints: (1) to say that the *first interpretation* contains *"elements of the full meaning"* is to say that the Lord Jesus Christ's resurrection body was not real or corporeal but *spiritualized* in some way. There was never any *"spiritualizing of the Lord's Peson."* (2) To say that Christ's *"ascending up"* refers to the *"cross"* is ridiculous on the face of it. The Lord said *"ascend up where he was before"* and He most certainly was *never* on the *"cross . . . before."* Here is an obvious desire to escape the literal, physical, bodily *ascension* of the Lord Jesus Christ into heaven by Westcott, which is *heresy.*

5. Westcott denied that *"the Son of Man"* was *"necessarily identified"* with *"the Christ"* in his understanding. He wrote:

(John 12:34) (who is this Son of man?) The question *clearly shews* that the *title "the Son of Man" was not necessarily identified with "the Christ."*

—Westcott—*John, op. cit.,* p. 184

Here is a clear place especially where the *heresy* of Westcott appears in regard to the *Person* and *natures* of the Lord Jesus Christ. He is very fuzzy and double-minded in his treatment of the natures of Christ—splitting them into various compartments as he does throughout his writings—but here he comes out and denies that there is an *essential* and a *"necessary identification"* between *"the Son of Man"* and *"the Christ."* This separation of *"the Son of Man"* and *"the Christ,"* as if there are *two persons* represented (like the Christian Scientistsl) is *heresy.* He is one and the Same *Person.*

6. Westcott furhter *splits* and *dissects* the *Person* of the Lord Jesus Christ into *"Jesus"* and *"the Christ."* He wrote:

> (Hebrews 5:5) (So Christ (the Christ) also . . .) It is *not* said that *"Jesus"* glorified not Himself, but *"the Christ,"* the appointed Redeemer, glorified not Himself.
> —Westcott—*Hebrews, op. cit.,* p. 122

The Bible knows of no such dissection of the *Person of the Son of the* Lord Jesus Christ. *"Jesus"* was every bit the *"Appointed Redeemer"* as was *"the Christ,"* since they are one and the same *Person,* and cannot be arbitrarily divided up as apostate Westcott and apostate Hort seek to do repeatedly in their books. This is *heresy.* Matthew 1:21 says clearly: "And she shall bring forth a son, and thou shalt call His name *Jesus:* for He shall *save his people from their sins."* It was *"Jesus"* who was to *"save"* and to *"redeem,"* and Westcott has no biblical grounds whatsoever for this heretical bifurcation of the theanthropic *God-Man Person* of the Lord Jesus Christ.

7. Westcott wrongly implied that Christ prayed to be delivered or have *"victory over death"* which was the *"fruit of sin."* He wrote:

> (Hebrews 5:7) The question has been asked for what did Christ pray? . . . Perhaps it is *best to answer* generally, *for the victory over death the fruit of sin.*
> —Westcott—*Hebrews, op. cit.,* p. 126

The Lord Jesus Christ *always* had the victory over *death*, and he didn't have to pray for this. As the ever-living One, the Creator of the universes, He had no problem with *death*. He could have been praying, on the contrary, to be spared dying in the Garden of Gethsemane rather than at the cross where He knew He must pay for the sins of the world. But the *sad* implication here is that somehow *"death"* also was the fruit of *"sin"* which might have been His own. This implication, however slight, should never have been present.

8. Hort wrongly implied that *"Christ"* was not *"God."* Hort wrote, as noted before also:

> (Revelation 1:2) . . . John's conveyance of the revelation to the churches, just as he had received it from the angel, and the angel from *Christ*, and *Christ* from *God*.
>
> —Hort—*Revelation, op. cit.*, p. 7

As we had discussed above, Hort rejected the idea that the Lord Jesus Christ, first of all, was the prime Revealer of Revelation, and secondly, that Christ was not *"God,"* since He got His revelation from *"God."* The use of *"God the Father,"* *"God the Son,"* and *"God the Holy Spirit,"* would be much, much clearer, that is, *if* Westcott and/or Hort *really* believed that all Three were really *"God."*

H. Westcott is confused about the various names of the Lord Jesus Christ, like *"Lord," "Jesus"* and *"Christ,"* wrongly dividing the Person of Christ.

1. Westcott wrongly refers to the Lord Jesus Christ's *"Divine personality"* rather than to the *God-Man Person* with the two separate natures in one *Person.* He wrote:

> (Hebrews 1:4) (being made a little lower than the an-
> gels) They also rightly point out that it is used of the *Lord's*
> Human Nature and *not of His divine personality. . . .*
>
> —Westcott—*Hebrews, op. cit.,* p. 17

First, I don't know what Westcott means by *"divine,"* since
he uses this to apply to human beings such as we are, and not
exclusively to *Deity* or to *God.* This is, in and of itself a weak
expression. Second, the Lord Jesus Christ did *not* have a *"divine personality."* He had a *human nature* and He had a *nature of Deity* or a *God-nature* or, in Westcott's words (defining
them as equal to *Deity* and *God*), He had a *divine nature.* He
had but *one Person,* and that one *Person* was the combination
of *Deity* and *humanity,* of *God* and *man,* of theos and anthro-
pos. To use the word *"personality"* which sounds like *"person"* when what might be meant would be *"nature"* is confusing in the extreme. Third, since there was a *hypostatic union*
of the *God-Man* natures into *one Person,* what happened to
the *one* nature, happened to the other nature from the stand-
point of "being made a little lower than the angels." The *Person* is *one.* This temporary state, pending His resurrection,
when He ascended far up above all principality and powers
and higher than the angels, was a state, by virtue of the Incarnation, of the entire *God-Man Person* of the Lord Jesus
Christ.

**2. Westcott uses the *names* of the Lord Jesus Christ as a
tool to divide up His *Person* arbitrarily like the Christian
Science people wrongly do today.** He wrote:

> Speaking (Hebrews 1:4) generally we may say that Jesus
> directs our thoughts to His *human nature,* Christ to His
> Work as the Fulfiller of the old Dispensation, Son to His
> *divine nature,* Lord itself to His sovereignty over the Church.

1. Of these Names that which is distinctive of the Epistle is the *human name, Jesus.*

—Westcott—*Hebrews, op. cit.,* p. 33

There is no warrant from Scripture whatsoever to speak of *"Jesus"* as being the Lord Jesus Christ's *"human name."* He is ever and always the *God-Man.* He is *Deity* combined (but not confused) with *humanity.* Regardless of His many *titles* or *names,* they each and every one of them carry with them His full credentials as both *Deity* and *humanity.* This is true whether the name is *"Lord,"* or *"Jesus,"* or *"Christ,"* or *"Son of Man,"* or *"Son of God,"* or *"Alpha,"* or *"Omega,"* or *"the Lily of the Valley,"* or any of the scores of other names given to the Savior in the Bible. Matthew 1:21, I remind you, spoke of the name *"Jesus"* because He would *"save his people from their sins."* There is nothing more depicting *Deity* or *God* Himself than *"saving people from sins."* In fact, none but God could accomplish such a feat. This is no more a *human* name of the Lord Jesus Christ than any other of His Names. Westcott seems to demean the Savior throughout his writings consulted by being able to use *"Jesus"* as merely the *"human name"* and thus not conveying His *Deity/humanity Person.* By whatever name is used, the entire *Person* of the Lord Jesus Christ is conveyed. He cannot be *dissected* or *divided* up by names used for Him. Westcott does the same for *"Jesus"* on page 74 (Hebrews 3:2), and on page 164 (Hebrews 6:20), and again in 1 Peter 5:5 (*op. cit.,* p. 180). In all of these passages, he cites the words *"the human name, Jesus."*

The Heresies of Westcott and Hort
on the *Work* of the Lord Jesus Christ.

A. *Westcott* explained away *some of the* miracles *of the Lord Jesus Christ* by downplaying or omitting the literal phase of the miracle.

(John 6:21) It will be obvious that these two *"signs"* are introductory to the discourse which follows. Both correct *limited views* springing out of our *material conceptions*. Effects are produced at variance with our ideas of quantity and quality. That which is *small* becomes *great*. That which is *heavy* moves on the *surface of the water.* Contrary elements yield at a divine presence. Both *"signs"* in other words, prepare the way for *new thoughts* of Christ, of His sustaining, preserving, guiding power, and *exclude deductions drawn from corporeal relations only.* He can support men, though visible means fall short. He is with His disciples, though they do not recognize or see Him. . . .

—Westcott—*John, op. cit.,* p. 99

This sounds like a modernistic *apostate* explaining away the *miracles* alluded to above. He wants to de-emphasize *"material conceptions"* and *"exclude"* completely any *"deductions drawn from corporeal relations only."* Thus the *literalness* of these *miracles* is suspected and bypassed by Westcott, in favor of a *spiritualization* of them.

(John 11:25) The *resurrection* is *not* a doctrine but a fact: *not future but present:* not multitudinous, but belonging to the *unbroken continuity of each separate life.* . . . I am—*not I shall be hereafter*—I AM. . . .

—Westcott—*John, op. cit.,* p. 168

Here is Westcott's flat denial of the *future resurrection*, holding only to some sort of undefined, *spiritualized "present"* form.

B. Westcott and Hort deny or have a false meaning to the literal, bodily resurrection *of the Lord Jesus Christ, and remain in general*.

1. Westcott falsely thought the *"resurrection of Christ"* was the *"restoration"* of the *"Tabernacle of God's presence to men."* He wrote:

> (John 2:19) Destroy this temple, and in three days I will raise it up) On the other hand the *resurrection of Christ* was the raising again of the Temple, the complete *restoration of the Tabernacle of God's presence to men*, perpetuated in the *church, which is Christ's body.*
>
> —Westcott—*John, op. cit.*, p. 42

All Westcott the *apostate* and *heretic* has for the bodily *resurrection of our* Lord Jesus Christ is the *"restoration of . . . God's presence to men"* which is *"perpetuated in the church, which is Christ's body."* Just so there is a *visible church*, for Westcott, there is a *resurrection. Heresy*, pure and simple, and *ugly*.

2. Westcott falsely thought Christ's body passed through *"earthly dissolution"* in his wrong view of the resurrection. He wrote:

> (Hebrews 7:16) The *life of Christ* was not endless or eternal only. It was essentially *"indissoluble"* (Ajkatavlupto). Although the form of its manifestation was changed and in the earthly sense He died, yet His life endured unchanged even through *earthly dissolution. . . .*
>
> —Westcott—*Hebrews, op. cit.*, p. 185

There was *no "earthly dissolution"* of the body of the Lord Jesus Christ, because He *"saw no corruption."* His body was literally and physically *resurrected* from the dead, and He is still at the Father's right hand to this very hour, as the *"man, Christ Jesus,"* raised bodily, ascended bodily, seated bodily at the Right Hand of God the Father, and coming one day *bodily* as He promised.

3. Hort wrongly *spiritualized* the *resurrection* from the dead in 1 Peter 1:3. He wrote:

> (1 Peter 1:3) (by the *resurrection of Jesus Christ from the dead*) How our Lord's Resurrection was the *instrument by* which a new life of hope was brought into mankind may be read in many places of the Acts and the Epistles. It reversed every doom of every kind of death, and thus annulled the hopelessness which must settle down on every one who thinks out seriously what is involved in the universal empire of death. It was by the faith in the Resurrection that *mankind was enabled to renew its youth.*
>
> —Hort--*1 Peter, op. cit.,* p. 34

This is a *spiritualization* of the resurrection. It doesn't *"enable" "mankind"* to *"renew its youth."* It teaches that every born-again believer will one day receive a *new body*, physically raised from the dead or transformed instantaneously from a *mortal* body to an *immortal* body at His Coming. Hort knows *nothing* of this glorious *hope*, but spiritualizes it away to *nothingness.*

C. *Westcott refused to stand for* "propositions about Christ," *thinking that it was all right just simply to* "believe" "in Christ," *whoever He might be.*

> (John 14:1) (believe also in me) The *belief* is *"in Christ,"* and *not in any propositions about Christ.*
>
> —Westcott—*John, op. cit.,* p. 200

This may sound all well and good, but just *how,* pray tell, can you believe *"in Christ"* if you don't have the slightest idea about just *who* He is, based on the Bible, and all of its definite *"propositions about Christ"*? This is the chief *heresy* of Westcott, that is, his disdain to be pinned down to *'propositions about Christ."* He has passed on this *heresy* to many, many twentieth century people today as well, sad to say.

D. *Westcott was very* heretical *concerning the* "Second Coming" *of the Lord Jesus Christ.*

1. Westcott *heretically* believed in many different *"comings"* of the Lord Jesus Christ in John 14:3. He wrote:

> (John 14:3) (. . . I will come again, and receive you unto myself;) But though the words refer to the *last "coming" of Christ,* the promise *must not be limited to that one "coming"* which is the consummation of all *comings."* Nor again must it be confined to the *"coming" to the church on the day of Pentecost,* or to the *"coming" to the individual either at conversion or at death,* though these *"comings"* are included in the thought. Christ is in fact from the moment of His Resurrection *ever coming to the world and to the church, and to men,* as the Risen Lord (Comp. i. 9). This thought is expressed by the use of the present *I come,* as distinguished from the future *I will come,* as of one *isolated future act.* The *"coming" is regarded in its continual present* . . . side by side with *this constant coming. . . .*
>
> —Westcott—*John, op. cit.,* p. 201

This comment, for those who know the Bible on the Second Coming of the Lord Jesus Christ, needs no further elaboration by me. Its *heresies* are obvious. For Westcott, words don't mean anything. He can make them whatever he might wish to make of them. Many *modernist apostates* and *heretics* of today have followed his lead here, especially including John MacArthur who changes *"blood"* to mean merely *"death."* For a full discussion on this, see my book, *John MacArthur's Heresy on the Blood of Christ* (**#2185 @ $5.00+$3.00 S&H**).

2. Westcott repeats similar errors concerning the Second Coming of the Lord Jesus Christ throughout his works. He refers the Second Coming to the coming of the Holy Spirit (cf. Westcott—*John*, *op. cit.*, John 14:16, p. 205); he speaks of *"several comings of Christ"* (cf. Westcott—*1–3 John, op. cit.*, 1 John 2:18, p. 69); he refers to the expression, *"as often as Christ comes"* (cf. Westcott—*1–3 John*, *op. cit.*, 1 John 2:18, p. 71); He says that *"He is still coming"* in the *"flesh"* (cf. Westcott—*1–3 John*, *op. cit.*, 1 John 4:2, p. 142); and he refers to a *"continuous spiritual coming"* of Christ (cf. Westcott—*1–3 John*, *op. cit.*, 1 John 5:6, p. 182). These all perpetuate Westcott's *heresy* in this vital department of Christology.

E. Westcott and Hort had a false and heretical view of the vicarious, substitutionary sacrifice of the Lord Jesus Christ.

1. Westcott believed the *heresy* that the *"redemptive efficacy"* of *"Christ's work"* was found *"in His whole life,"* rather than in His death. He wrote:

> (John 1:29) (which taketh away the sin of the world) The parallel passage in the Epistle (l.c.) shews that the *redemptive efficacy of Christ's word* is to be *found in His whole life....*
>
> —Westcott—*John, op. cit.*, p. 20

Here is a verse, John 1:29, which shows that the *"Lamb of God"* took away the sin of the world by His offering on the cross, and yet Westcott used it to show *"redemptive efficacy"* is found *"in His whole life."* This is nothing short of blatant *heretical* modernistic *apostasy.* Jesus Christ's *life* did not nor could not *redeem* us. It was only the *shedding of His blood* at the cross which is the basis of man's redemption.

2. Westcott wrongly thought John 6:51 did *not* speak of Christ's *"atonement."* He wrote:

> (John 6:51) (my flesh) The thought here is of support and growth, and *not of atonement.*
>
> —Westcott—*John, op. cit.,* p. 106

The whole importance of the teachings in this section of John 6 has to do with the *"atonement"* of the Lord Jesus Christ. How else can we understand His giving us His *"flesh"* to eat?

3. Westcott wrongly took Christ's *"flesh"* in John 6:51 to be *"the virtue of His humanity.* He wrote:

> (John 6:51, 53) It is not yet indicated how the *"flesh"* of Christ, *the virtue of His humanity,* will be communicated to and made effectual for mankind or men. . . . By the *"flesh"* in this narrower sense we must understand the *virtue of Christ's humanity* as living for us; by the *"blood"* the *virtue of His humanity* as subject to death.
>
> —Westcott—*John, op. cit.,* pp. 106–07

Christ's *"flesh"* is *"communicated to and made effectual for mankind or men"* by His crucifixion on the cross. Westcott has misdefined and *spiritualized* both *"flesh"* and *"blood,"* rather than taking them literally to refer to what was accomplished on the cross for lost men.

4. Westcott *heretically* declared that throughout Christ's *"last discourses"* the *"redemptive work of Christ essentially was completed."* He wrote:

(John 13:31) (glorified) The thought throughout these *last discourses* is of the decisive act by which the Passion had been embraced. *The redemptive work of Christ essentially was completed* (xvii. 4, etc.).

—Westcott—*John, op. cit.,* p. 196

By *no means* was the *"redemptive work of Christ"* either *"essentially completed"* or even partly *completed* while He was giving His *"last discourses."* This harks back to Westcott's *heresy* that Christ's *"whole life"* has *"redemptive efficacy"* (cf. 5 'a' above).

5. Westcott gave *"plausibility"* and *"authority"* to the false *"cause of the death of Christ"* as a *"rupture of the heart"* rather than the biblical cause. He wrote:

(John 19:34) (blood and water) It has been argued (*with the greatest plausibility and authority* by Dr. Stroud, "The physical cause of the Death of Christ," ed. 2, 1871) that this is a natural phenomenon. The *immediate cause of death was* (it is said) *a rupture of the heart. . . .*

—Westcott—*John, op. cit.,* p. 279

No. The *"immediate cause of death"* was the fact that the Lord Jesus Christ *dismissed His Spirit.* He simply said, *"into thy hands I commend my spirit"* and so gave up His Spirit and died physically. This was the cause of death. It was a *miracle* of Deity which no human being is capable of performing. If a *physical cause* of death can be found (other than the biblical one), then how can we be sure He didn't die an "accidental death" and that He did *not* atone for the sins of the world in His sacrifice? John 10:18 is clear on this point.

6. Westcott wrongly said that *"death"* rather than the *"shedding of the blood"* is the *"seal"* of the validity of a covenant. He wrote:

(Hebrews 9:14) *Death* again, which makes the *blood available,* is the *seal* of the validity of a covenant.
>   —Westcott—*Hebrews, op. cit.,* p. 261

No. *"Death"* in and of itself is *not* the *"seal"* of the Covenant, but, on the contrary, it is the *"shedding of the blood"* which is the *"seal"* of the New Covenant and all biblical covenants. *"Death"* could be by natural causes, and without any *shedding of blood* whatsoever, and that would not *"seal"* anything. Again, here John MacArthur continues this heresy.

7. Westcott had a wrong view of *"blood"* as the *"idea of life"* rather than *"death."* He wrote:

(Hebrews 9: 12) I have endeavoured to shew elsewhere (Addit. Note on 1 John 1:7) that the Scriptural idea of *blood* is *essentially* an *idea of life* and *not of death.*
>   —Westcott—*Hebrews, op, cit.,* p. 293

This is foreign to the Bible's usage. *"Blood"* is ever used in sacrifices, and is ever spoken of as being *"shed."* This *shedding of blood* can hardly speak of *"life,"* but is a picture of the *"death"* of the sacrifice.

8. Westcott wrongly believed the *"offering of the body of Jesus Christ once for all"* somehow *"slowly matured through life."* He wrote:

(Hebrews 10:10) (through the offering of the body of Jesus Christ once for all) Through the offering of the body divinely prepared, *which offering, slowly matured through life,* was consummated on the cross.
>   —Westcott—*Hebrews, op. cit.,* p. 312

If this *"offering"* was indeed *"once for all,"* [and it *was,* at the cross], how could it be *"slowly matured through life"*? This again is pure *apostate heresy.*

9. Westcott wrongly taught that *"redemption, forgiveness, atonement"* and *"reconciliation"* came through Christ's *"incarnation," "life," "passion,"* and *"resurrection,"* rather than just through His *sacrifice at Calvary*. He wrote:

> (Hebrews 10:10) He requires *redemption, forgiveness, atonement, reconciliation.* All these blessings Christ has brought to humanity by His *incarnation,* His *life,* His *passion,* His *ascension.*
>
> —Westcott—*Hebrews, op. cit.,* p. 344

All of these great spiritual gifts and benefits—*redemption, forgiveness, atonement,* and *reconciliation*—came from the sacrifice of the Lord Jesus Christ at Calvary, and not a single one came from His *"life,"* or *"incarnation"* only, or even *"ascension."* Here is Westcott's downplaying once more the sacrifice of Christ and His shedding of His blood at the cross. It is *heresy.*

10. Hort denies that in 1 Peter 1:2, there is no *"reference"* to the idea of *"ransom"* in the words, *"sprinkling of the blood of Jesus Christ."* He wrote:

> (1 Peter 1:2) In the N.T. the *blood of Christ* is associated with various images which need to be clearly distinguished. There is here *no direct reference* to the idea of *purchase or ransom,* as in vv. 18.19 . . . or to the ideal of *sacrificial atonement,* as in several other books of the N.T.
>
> —Hort—*1 Peter, op. cit.,* p. 23

Hort is *heretical* here again. There is no reference to the *"blood of Jesus Christ"* in the New Testament which does not refer and relate directly to *"purchase,"* or *"ransom,"* or *"sacrificial atonement."*

11. Hort failed to find the reference to the *"blood of unblemished and unspotted lamb"* as a reference to the *Lord Jesus Christ*, the *Lamb of God*. He wrote:

> (1 Peter 1:19) (But with the precious blood of Christ, as of a lamb without blemish and without spot) In this allusion to the *blood of an unblemished and unspotted lamb*, what had St Peter in mind? Chiefly, I think, and perhaps *solely* the paschal lamb.
>
> —Hort—*1 Peter, op. cit.*, p. 77

There is no mystery nor wonder as to the reference to this *"Lamb"* to the simplest believer—and it is *not* to the *"paschal"* or *"passover"* lamb of Exodus 12. It is to the *"Lamb of God"* who taketh away the sin of the world (John 1:29). What a pity that the *heresies* of *Hort* preclude his discernment of spiritual verities in this. Hort holds that the "paschal lamb" is in view later in the discussion as well (Cf. 1 Peter, *op. cit.*, p. 79) in connection with the same verse.

12. Hort stated that Christ's *"precious blood"* in 1 Peter 1:19 is only *"figurative language"* as a *"ransom."* He wrote:

> (1 Peter 1:19) The true lesson is that the *language* which speaks of a *ransom is but figurative language.* . . .
>
> —Hort—*1 Peter, op. cit.*, p. 80

In other words, Hort holds to the *heresy* that the blood atonement of the Lord Jesus Christ really didn't take place *literally*, but the whole idea of redemption through Christ's *"precious blood"* is all *"figurative."* If such be the case, then *Hort* is in *Hell* today. This heresy has been popularized in our days by John MacArthur. The reader is urged to get my book, *John MacArthur's Heresy on the Blood of Christ*. It is **BFT #2185** @ **$5.00 + $3.00** for S&H.

Chapter XI

Summary and Conclusions

Though a great many things could be said at the conclusion of this brief analysis of the *theological heresies of Westcott and Hort,* this brief *summary,* followed by some *conclusions* will be suggestive only, in an effort to tie together into one small space some of the more outstanding pieces of the *heretical* puzzle known throughout the entire civilized world as *"Westcott and Hortism."*

A. Summary

Chapter I discussed such background information as why study Westcott and Hort's *heresies;* what the significance is if they had *heresies;* their *heresis* in contrast with John Burgon's soundness; the five books studied and quoted from throughout the analysis; the plan of treatment used; and what would be included in the study.

Chapter II included a discussion of Westcott and Hort's *heresies* in the area of *bibliology* or the Bible, including wrong views on *inspiration;* on *biblical interpretation;* on *Israel and the Church;* and on *incomplete exegesis* of vital verses.

Chapter III took up Westcott and Hort's *heresies* in the area
of *theology proper,* or the doctrine of God, including the
Fatherhood of God; a denial that Christ made known *God;*
and a denial of God's being *propitiated.*

Chapter IV included Westcott and Hort's *heresies* in the area
of *anthropology* and *hamartiology,* or the doctrines of *man*
and of *sin,* including teaching that *men could be divine;*
*evolution; man's perfectability; a heretical view of psychol-
ogy of man;* and other matters.

Chapter V included Westcott and Hort's *heresies* in the area
of *Satanology* or the doctrine of *Satan,* including their
failure to affirm his *personality.*

Chapter VI included Westcott and Hort's *heresies* in the area
of *ecclesiology* or the doctrine of the *Church,* including a
confusion of Christ's literal *body,* with the *"body of Christ"*
which is the *Church universal;* and *baptismal regeneration.*

Chapter VII included Westcott and Hort's *heresies* in the area
of *pneumatology* or the doctrine of the *Holy Spirit,* including their false view of *the Holy Spirit at Christ's baptism;* a failure to recognize the *indwelling of the Holy Spirit
in the believer;* and a false reference to *"a Holy Spirit."*

Chapter VIII included Westcott and Hort's *heresies* in the
area of *eschatology* or the doctrine of future things, including their false views of *heaven and eternal life; spiritualization of the "second death"; post-millennialism;* and
the *non-literal view of Christ's Second Coming.*

Chapter IX included Westcott and Hort's *heresies* in the area
of *soteriology* or the doctrine of *salvation,* including the
false view that Christ's *"whole life"* had *"redemptive efficacy"; universalism;* and a false view of *eternal life.*

Chapter X was the *major chapter,* and included Westcott and
Hort's *heresies* in the area of *Christology* or the doctrine

of *Christ,* including:

A. *Heresies on the **person** of Christ,* such as: error on the *pre-existence of Christ;* on the *omniscience of Christ;* on the *omnipresence of Christ;* on the *Deity of Christ;* on the *impeccability or sinlessness of Christ;* on the *person and natures of Christ;* and on the *names of Christ.* It also included

B. *Heresies on the **work** of Christ,* such as: error on the *miracles of Christ;* on the *bodily resurrection of Christ;* on *propositions about Christ;* on the *Second Coming of Christ;* and on the *vicarious substitutionary sacrifice of Christ.*

Chapter XI included a *summary* and *conclusions* in regard to the *heresies of Westcott and Hort.*

B. Conclusions

1. **Westcott and Hort are *not "evangelicals"* in theology, but in reality are *"apostates"* and *"heretics."*** If one thing is certain, after the careful reading of the foregoing 125 *quotations* from the *five books* (c. 1,291 pages in all: 1,056 from Westcott, and 235 from Hort), Westcott and Hort are *not* the cool, careful, sound, *fundamentalist* or *evangelical* writers they have always been passed off to being. Instead, they are *apostate* and *heretical* in many, many vital areas and doctrines of the historical Christian faith as taught in the Bible. These 125 *quotations* are not *all* such quotations, but are merely a *sampling* of the quotations that could be cited. These were given in the interests of *time* and *space* and at the same time attempted to give *substance to this* conclusion of the *non-evangelicalism* of Westcott and Hort. Though there might be some slight room for difference of opinion and interpretation of a few of these 125 *quotations,* there are still enough

left when you're finished to make quite a *convincing* array of *evidence* against their *fundamentlaism.*

It is amazing to me to have Dr. Stewart Custer of Bob Jones University defend Westcott and Hort's orthodoxy in his book, *The Truth About the King James Version.* The whole story is told in *The Life and Letters of Westcott* (**BFT #1866 @ $45.00 + $5.00 S&H**) and in *The Life and Letters of Hort* (**BFT #1867 @ $48.00 + $5.00 S&H**). It is also amazing that Theodore Letis likewise believes Westcott and Hort are conservatives in theology. Letis is a Lutheran who has been for many years pushing his way into fundamental and Baptist circles, even though he looks down on both groups. "There are none so blind as those who **will not** see."

2. **Since Westcott and Hort were *"heretics"* and *"apostates"* in so many of their theological areas, Bible-believers should be warned against them.** It is sad that so many *evangelicals* consider *Westcott and Hort* as being *"evangelicals"* and thorough-going Bible-believers, when the *reverse* is true. Bible-believing Christians therefore should be *warned* against the apostasy of these men so that *if* they get their books, they will not accept everything they write as being from a sound expositor.

3. **Since Westcott and Hort were *heretical* in so many areas, their *veracity* on their *theories* of New Testament *textual criticism* cannot be trusted.** Any men who would twist the Bible's clear meanings as Westcott and Hort have done in these above areas, cannot be trusted in any other biblical area as well. The Westcott and Hort *theory* of New Testament textual criticism which has dominated the field since the production of the English Revised Version (ERV) of 1881, based on their *false Greek text,* cannot be accepted on face value, because the perpetrators of such a the-

ory have been proven to be deceivers and *apostates* and *heretics* in so many other areas of Bible doctrine. If these men would deceive and pervert the Bible so much in these areas which we have examined in the foregoing pages, what is to prevent them from putting over on the world a fictitious and *error-filled* theory of New Testament textual criticism? The book by Wilbur N. Pickering [*The Identity of the New Testament Text*, **BFT #556**, available from BFT for a gift of **$12.00 + $3.00 S&H**] shows very clearly that many of the things claimed by Westcott and Hort in their New Testament textual criticism were just *not true*. In fact, they *lied* about what they had done, out and out. It is easy for me to understand the *why* of their *lying*, now that we have seen so clearly that they are not true *evangelicals* or *fundamentalists* in their theology, but *heretics*. Their word cannot be trusted, therefore, and their motivation to twist and to doctor the New Testament Greek text to conform to their *heresies* is the more plausible under these circumstances.

4. **Since Westcott and Hort were *heretical* in many areas of Bible doctrine, *no part of their textual theory should be accepted without clear, positive proof.*** Once a man's theology is found to be *false*, his *word* can be *false* in any area whatsoever. No one should take *any part* of their textual theories without positive *proof* which is beyond question. You should *not* take their *"word for it,"* since they have lied about what they claim over and over again. In fact, it is high time for *fundamentalists* and any *evangelicals* as well, to (in view of the above analysis of the *heresies of Westcott and Hort* throw out the entire *Westcott and Hort* textual theories *lock, stock, and barrel* as being the work of blatant *heretics* and *apostates*. Since when do Bible-believing *fundamentalists* take *any* of their

theories or views of the Bible from proven *heretics?*

5. **With Westcott and Hort's** *heresies* **as mentioned above in this analysis, it is easier to understand why they treated the Bible like** *"any other book."* Without any sound *fundamentalism* in doctrine, why should the Bible be accepted as a *special book?* This is why Westcott and Hort claimed they were treating the Bible as any other book in their *naturalistic method* of textual criticism because they did not hold that it was plenarily and verbally inspired of God and hence inerrant and infallible in the original languages.

6. **With the above** *heresies* **held by Westcott and Hort, it would be** *impossible* **for them to have been** *saved men,* **and hence they are in hell today.** This realization of their *heresy* must bring with it the consequent realization that they are *not saved,* and hence they are in *hell today* for all eternity. This is a sobering fact. Though these men were high up in the *Anglican Church* of their day, they cannot use that to escape *hell.* They must be *"in Christ,"* having Him as their personal Savior and Lord to be in heaven. Since they refused to accept Him as the Bible pictures Him to be, they could not possibly have been saved.

7. **Since Westcott and Hort** *"bring not this doctrine"* **concerning the** *person and work* **of the Lord Jesus Christ, we should not** *"receive them"* **nor bid them** *"God-speed."* Second John 1:7–11 clearly teaches that when men come and do not bring the *"doctrine of Christ"* (v. 9), these men are *"deceivers"* and these men are *"anti-Christs"* (v.7). It is also true that these men who do not hold the biblical *"doctrine of or about Christ"* (such as Westcott and Hort, cf. pp. 21-37 above) do *not "have God"* (v. 9). Furthermore, it is told us clearly that when such men come around, we are not to *"receive"* them *"into your house,*

neither bid them God speed, for he that biddeth him God speed is partaker of their [his] *evil deeds"* (vv. 10–11). By application of this passage of Scripture, and in view of the *heretical Christology* of Westcott and Hort outlined above, we should not *"receive"* their New Testament textual theories or bid such theories *"God speed"* or else we are *"partakers of their evil deeds"* by extension.

A man's theories are influenced by the *beliefs* which he holds, and Westcott and Hort and their theories are no exception. This is a dire and serious warning which is needed today more than ever before. When the *Westcott and Hort* false theory of textual criticism is revered and almost *"worshipped"* even in our *fundamentalists'* and *separatists'* Bible institutes, colleges, and theological seminaries, the facts and the truth of their *heresies* should be circulated in all quarters of the Bible-believing world. To this end, please send your *gifts* to *The Bible for Today* of **$4.00 each + $3.00 S&H** for as many copies as possible to be *mailed* to the schools, pastors, and friends of your choice so that they might be aware of these *heresies* on the part of *Westcott and Hort.* You may have **two copies** for a *gift* of **$7.00 (+ $3.00 S&H)** to *The Bible for Today.* Postage will help to send these to the people and/or schools of your choice. Can you help us in this endeavor?

8. The *battle* against *Westcott and Hort's false textual theory will* be waged throughout the coming decades and your Bible and its *true texts are at stake.* The importance of *Westcott and Hort* historically in the false theories of textual criticism that they initiated cannot be forgotten. It is of utmost importance to the *true text* of the Bible to oppose their *Minority Greek Text* and to *support* the *Traditional Greek Text* which is the text underlying the King James Version of the New Testament. Let's not allow these

two *unbelieving heretics* to ruin and to spoil our Bibles. Have they not done enough by their *heresies* as outlined in this analysis? Do we need them to use their influence beyond the grave to gain support and respectability to their false text of the New Testament? This is a deadly and an important battle, and it will not be an easy one to win, but *The Bible for Today* will persist in its efforts to support the *Traditional Greek Text* of the New Testament and *oppose* the false and defective *heretical text* of Westcott and Hort constructed to accommodate their own *biblical heresies*. For a complete list of *materials* (pamphlets, books, and booklets) both by yours truly, and by many other authors who also are *opposed* to the *Westcott and Hort* false text of the New Testament, write us for a *Caalog of Publications*, and then look in the *index* under *"Bible"* part *"K"* to find the many, many helpful publications on this vital subject which we carry in *The Bible for Today*. Presently, we have over one thousand titles defending the King James Bible and its underlying Hebrew and Greek texts. Get my *Defending the King James Bible* (**BFT #1594-P @ $12.00 + $3.00 S&H**) for more information.

9. **Westcott and Hort's *heresies* in doctrine *completely cancel* any so-called *"scholarship"* which many feel they had.** I've often heard the argument in *favor of Westcott and Hort* to the effect that *"they were certainly tremendous scholars."* But even *if* this were the case (and I am not prepared even to concede this point without a more thorough examination of it; in fact I am prone to *doubt* this fact very much having studied their phony textual theories of the New Testament Greek Text), do not their *heresies* completely *overrule* any such *"scholarship"*? I think that this is the case. First Corinthians 2:14 clearly states that the *"natural man,"* such as *Westcott and Hort* were,

cannot *"receive"* the things *"of the Spirit of God,"* for they
are *"foolishness unto him: neither can he know them, because they are spiritually discerned."* What good is *"scholarship"* (if they even had it) if you can't *"understand"* or
"discern" the subject-matter of your study? And such is
the case with these *heretics,* Westcott and Hort. Their un-
saved *natural minds* could not begin to *comprehend* the
things of *"the Spirit of God,"* but they were *"foolishness
unto them."*

Index of Certain Words and Phrases

[NOTE: The phrases used in this *index* might be used by other speakers, and are not necessarily the opinions of the author of this study. DAW]

Index of Scripture References

About the Author

The author of this book, Dr. D. A. Waite, received a B.A. degree in classical Greek and Latin from the University of Michigan in 1948, a Th.M. degree, with high honors, in New Testament Greek Literature and Exegesis from Dallas Theological Seminary in 1952, an M.A. degree in Speech from Southern Methodist University in 1953, a Th.D., with honors, in Bible Exposition from Dallas Theological Seminary in 1955, and a Ph.D. in Speech from Purdue University in 1961. He holds both New Jersey and Pennsylvania teacher certificates in Greek and Language Arts.

He has been a teacher in the areas of Greek, Hebrew, Bible, Speech, and English for over thirty-five years in nine schools, including one junior high, one senior high, three Bible institutes, two colleges, two universities, and one seminary. He served his country as a Navy chaplain for five years on active duty; pastored two churches; was chairman and director of the Radio and Audio-Film Commission of the American Council of Christian Churches; since 1971, has been founder, president, and director of *The Bible for Today;* since 1978, has been president of the *Dean Burgon Society;* has produced over 700 other studies, books, cassettes, or video cassettes on various topics; and is heard on both a five-minute daily and thirty-minute weekly radio program *In Defense of Traditional Bible Texts,* presently on 25 stations.

Dr. and Mrs. Waite have been married since 1948; they have four sons, one daughter, and, at present, eight grandchildren.